ONLY BEGOTTEN

An Incredible Three Day Saga.

Inspired by actual events that

test reality and brings insanity

a sleepless night away.

Douglas Ware

Hold fast to dreams for if dreams die like a

broken winged bird that cannot fly

Hold fast to dreams for when dreams go life is a

barren field frozen with snow.

Dreams   Langston Hughes

If one advances confidently in the direction

of his dreams and endeavors to live the life

which he has imagined he will meet with a

success unexpected in the common hours.

Henry David Thoreau

Introduction

It has not rained in Los Angeles for months. The bone drying drought continues. Out of nowhere appears this crazy torrential freak rain storm. It's December. It looks like a late July tropical gulf coast storm in Mississippi.

I see someone trapped in the roaring L A River. The concrete river that normally looks like a trickle of water down someone's drive way. Yes! That's a little boy in the river, and at night of all times. The water is rushing him so fast as waves wash over him. It is so dark it's hard to keep him in sight. He looks about the size of a 10-year-old boy. His face reflects shear panic, fear, and confusion. What's going to happen to him? Who is with him? Aren't they trying to rescue him? Oh no! There is a huge tree that has fallen into the river rumbling towards him. Seems like the water is rushing faster and faster. The tree just overcame him pushing him under water. I can't see him. He is under the dark black water. The tree rushes on in the river. Suddenly, the boy is bobbing on a large branch but still trapped in this flash flood. He can't survive this. He is going to drown. He will die.

Suddenly a loud booming thunder crash shakes the ground. Followed by a flash of electric blue lightening. The doomed boy is illuminated still clinging to the branch. But now he is trapped in a foamy swirling whirlpool filled with debris.

The boy is looking up with pleading eyes. He reaches upward with one hand straining as much as he can. He loses his hold sinking below the water into the whirlpool. How will he survive this? A crackle of lightening streaks across the dark moonless sky like skeleton fingerlings. Out of nowhere, the boy's head appears tangled in the branch and rubbish. His face is bloody from a gash at his hairline. He looks so pitiful, cold, and overwhelmed with fear.

The sound of the rat, tat, tat, of a LAPD rescue chopper swoops rapidly overhead. A very loud voice booms from a speaker on the chopper. But the booming words are in an indistinguishable foreign language. The same message keeps repeating over and over. The chopper makes a deep angled swing back towards the boy. It flashes a blinding search light on the water where the boy is still swirling helplessly. The sound is deafening as the chopper hesitates above the boy. The boy reaches up towards the chopper his lips mouthing silent words for help. His pleading is palpable.

The chopper lowers slowly increases the swirl of the water around the boy. The thrashing of the branch causes the boy to lose his grip again, but he grabs hold before going under. The chopper adjusts its position and rises higher above the pleading boy. While the chopper steadies above, a rescue harness begins to slowly lower. A louder messages blares from the chopper. The boy begins to frantically reach for the harness raising himself as much as possible. The harness is nearly within the boys reach as he stretches more, and more with his little fingers twitching to grasp the harness. He is so exhausted, but he puts forth his best effort to reach the harness. It's within his reach and he grabs hold, locking his arm at the elbow into the harness. There is time for him to position himself more securely with both arms in the harness, but he is reluctant to let go of the lock hold he has with one arm. He looks up toward the chopper directly over him with the bright search light illuminating the frightened face, wet with water, tears, and blood.

Slowly, the chopper begins to rise. It moves away from the whirlpool and then starts retrieving the rescue harness with the boy in tow. The boy begins to spin, and the harness stops the upward motion. The boy becomes frantic and tries grasping with both arms causing the harness to swing and spin uncontrollably. That loud foreign language messages stops abruptly. Then unexpectedly, the harness breaks and the boy falls back into the water. He sinks motionless with his arms upstretched. His face is expressionless as small bubbles stream from his nostrils. He sinks into the deep darkness of the water.

I can't move! I can't move! I feel paralyzed. I know I'm dreaming, but I can't move. I'm struggling to move to stop this awful dream. But I can't move. I can't move! I hear myself trying to speak, but I can't. Why can't I move? I'm dreaming but I know I'm dreaming. I see it, but I can't move so it will stop. It feels like a heavy invisible weight is holding me on my back. I'm struggling just to make a sound, just yell.

There! There! I'm awake. I jerk myself and sit up in the bed. I'm choking and coughing while I gasp for breath. My wife lying beside me, is startled by the choking and coughing. She sits up too and touches my bear back and I jump from the unexpected touch of her warm hand on my sweaty back.

I utter an unexpected awkward sound as if I'm a frightened girl. Zena looks at me with surprise and concern. The hand she touched me with is suspended in space just inch from my back. I don't know what to do. I'm just as shocked as Zena by my actions. I quickly jump up and move quickly to the bathroom. The quick change in temperature makes me shiver. My body is damp with sweat and the dream still consumes me.

"Mar. You OK? Marlon where you going baby? What's wrong Mar?"

"Nothing is wrong. I gotta go pee. Go back to sleep babe." I didn't know what was going on myself. So, I couldn't tell her anything. I didn't want to worry her and start this all over again. Not now. Not ever again. My throat is dry and feels raw. I'm guessing from the strain of trying so hard to speak, to scream what the hell! That dream was so stifling and felt so real. Damn! It was a nightmare. It felt like it controlled me. I couldn't move or speak.

I examine myself in the mirror turning my head from side to side. I look normal except that my eyes are slightly red. In my self-inspection I was asking myself the same question Zena asked? What is wrong? I shook my head side to side again, looking into my eyes saying nothing. Nothing is wrong with me. I lean my head under the faucet and swallow a few gulps of cold water and splashed my face and neck. As I stand up to look at myself in the mirror again, I want everything to be normal. It was just a stupid dream.

Damn! Zena is standing right behind me. We were both looking at my face. Her arms are crossed, and she looks both concerned and aggravated. I'm trapped. I don't want the barrage of questions I know she has.

"What was that Mar? ... Please don't say it was nothing. That scared me hearing you choking and gasping like that. It sounded like you were trying to say something. I'm just concerned baby." "I know it was different." Talking fast I said, it was just that heavy soul food we had at that new restaurant. "Remember, I tried everything, and I had two vodka tonics as well. It was probably that or just bad heart burn."

I'm doing my best to divert her attention away from thinking about the past. I don't want her to become the hovering social worker that she is with those messed up teenagers she sees in therapy. That explanation is not working. She didn't buy the soul food ploy. She knows I can eat nails with hot sauce and not have a problem.

She just keeps looking hard at me with those piercing eyes. Her eyes are what attracted me to her. They are so unusual in color. You see them and there are light, light shades of brown with soft yellow flecks. You could even call them golden. They're so mesmerizing. Her skin tone and hair are similar in color to her eyes. I always thought it was so unique and fascinating.

When we met in college all I could do was gaze into her eyes. I remember clearly the first day I saw those eyes. We met on the bus going to classes at the university. She was sitting on the long seat right behind the bus driver. I paid my fare and as I turned to find a seat I was struck by her just staring at me. I froze for a second not moving and the motion of the bus caused me to drop an arm load of books right at her feet. Embarrassed, to say the least, I stooped to pick up my books. I could feel her penetrating stare on the back of my head. I slowly looked up at her and she had the most infectious and friendly smile. Her eyes were smiling right along with her lips. I felt like she had melted into me. For sure not in a menacing way, but a peaceful serene sense.

After gathering my books. I sat across from her on the other long bench seat. Neither one of us said a word. I tried pretending to look out of the window. Trying to appear cool about the situation. I couldn't stop looking at her. She was the together one. She just kept right on smiling and looking at me. No pretense. No pretending. There was no question about it. She was flirting and wanted me to know it. I guess I looked shy and inept, but I just wasn't prepared for someone to be so open and friendly.

Right now, I want to turn around and face her, look in those eyes, and say Zena. Nothing is wrong with me. But she speaks before I do.

"OK Mar… Let's go back to bed my man. I want you to hold me in your arms, and rock me back to sleep." "All right my woman. Let's go." I hug her tight and embraced her passionately while grabbing her ass. I take her hand and lead her back to the bedroom and our rumpled bed. She immediately snuggles up into my arms, positioning her head on my chest. I wrapped my arms around her and hold her close to me. It feels comforting and unsettling at the same time. Neither of us was convincing with our loving comments of assurance. What else could we have said? Talking right now wouldn't lead to anything positive. "Goodnight, Marlon Lakestone. I love you babe." "Goodnight Mrs. Lakestone. I love you more. See you in the morning. Sweet dreams."

Damn! Why did I say sweet dreams? I gotta get control. I can't let this happen again. Please God. Help me. I stared up at the ceiling not feeling at all sleepy. Not ready to close my eyes for fear of what might be behind my eyelids.

I don't know how, but Zena is asleep already. I wished that I could do that. My mind never seems to stop processing. Analyzing this and then that. Going back questioning why I did that or why didn't I do this. It is so frustrating and aggravating. It makes me crazy. I wished that I could stop doing this to myself. Especially when I dredge up feelings and attach them to the thoughts causing me to feel guilty, sad, and victimized by people and situations. All of it a big mess of false shit seemingly real,

and I end up overwhelmed in a state of depression.

The First Day

Let us keep the dance of rain our fathers kept,

and tread our dreams beneath the jungle sky.

Arna Bontemps

I just can't stay in the bed punishing myself with a flood of thoughts. Dawn is still a little way off, but I gotta get up to start the day. I need the time to get ready for this day. Time to pull myself together after that nightmare. I can't fool myself. It does feel like the other time when I was so depressed and had unusual dreams. I can't face that again.

Not now. I'm feeling good about my music and things are starting to happen for me. I have to keep it together or Zena is going to start on me about having a career. A regular job like her. Like everybody else. But I'm not everybody. Yes, I want a career, but not how she defines it. I really know how much she loves me. How much she cares about me. That's why I try hard to avoid talking about dreams and depression. I don't want to hurt her or disappoint her. I love her just as much. I need her in my life.

I think that is why my mother and Zena are so close. She sees herself in Zena because of the music thing. My father wanted to put performing before a regular 8:00 to 5:00 job. Ma probably struggled with this. I'm sure about that. I can remember a lot of it. All the way back to that farm in Mississippi. We lived on my grandfather's farm way out in the sticks near some place called Holmes Mississippi. Hard to believe that Mississippi, strong hold of the segregated South and Jim Crow rule allowed anyone but a white man to own land way back then. There were a few black land owners and my grandfather had the deed to his land.

My father called my grandfather Pops. Everyone else did too. Pops was an original native to the land. Some called Indians. That's where we got the name Lakestone. His full name was Adam Lakestone, which made my father Adam Lakestone Jr. His mother, my great, great, grandmother Rebecca was a slave. They said she was very feeble and sickly. She grew up in slavery. It was hard on her according to stories about things that happened back then. My grandfather was of the Choctaw tribe. I can see Pops Lakestone now. Tall, muscular, strong jaw bone with full lips defining his face. His dark, brown eyes were full of wisdom. Up close you can see a gray-blueish ring around his pupils, a testament to the aging process. His skin was a dark rich umber clay color. The silver hair on his head hung on his shoulders. When he was working it was tied in a knot at the back of his head. Pops made sure we knew our family's history. Both Indian and African. He told us about how the white settlers came in and pushed the Choctaw off their land forcing them completely out of Mississippi. Large numbers of Choctaw died in this exodus. Ironically, Adam Lakestone Sr. was able to keep his land and paid a token nickel and received a signed legal deed for it. People repeat stories that have been passed around explaining how Pops did it. Some implied he used "magic Indian" powers that tricked the formidable white men in their own cruel manipulation and unjust laws.

Pops was so comfortable to be around. He was always so calm and compassionate. The only way you knew he was upset was when he started speaking in the Choctaw language. Ma would hush us whenever this happened. I called my mother Ma, but her name is Elizabeth. Dad called her Lizzie. When Pops was speaking she would say "be quite and pay attention. Show some respect." She felt that Pops was going to say something very profound and we all needed to hear it.

Speaking of all. Besides my parents and me, my father's sister, and her children, lived on the farm too. It was fun having my cousins to play with. Everybody worked on the farm. The best way to describe the farm was the way my father did. My father would say that his father Pops, had some land, some livestock, and some crops. Guess he didn't see it the way I did back then. Of course, there was a lot of hard work from the time the sun came up, until Pops sat down to light his tobacco. But I had so many good times there enjoying the wide-open spaces of the land Pops owned. Whenever I had a chance I would go exploring on the land. Many times, they would send one of my cousins out to find me. Most times I was found sitting next to the stream that runs through the land. I would throw rocks skipping them across the water, or I would just sit and stare at the water. My grandfather had a Choctaw word for doing this. I wished I could remember that word now. It was something about connecting to the spirit that lives within us.

The best time on the land was when the whole family went down to the stream for the day. We relaxed, cooked, and ate a full table of good food cooked right there. It was a time that Pops really enjoyed because it gave him time to remember the old ways. Pops stopped going down to the stream one year when something happened to the water. Pops said it was bad and wouldn't let anyone go to the stream. Much later I found out that some modern farm work way up stream caused the water to become polluted. I hated that we didn't have our family gatherings there any longer. I would still sneak off by myself to sit beside the water and just lose myself in dreams.

Back on the land it seems like the only time my father was happy was when he was playing the piano. We had an old upright piano in the living room. During the hot summer months, he would roll it out on the front porch. After he had worked hard in the fields and took care of the cattle he would sit at the piano on the porch in the cool of the evening and stroke the keys with such conviction and effort. This was the time Pops' age had slowed him down and he stopped physically working the land. Pops still lit his tobacco, but it was when my father was playing the piano on the porch. Pops sat next to him in his old wicker rocker, eyes closed puffing his pipe with contentment.

I sat on the piano bench with my father. His fingers danced across striking the keys making the music as I imagined I was too. I watched his fingers moving very closely, while moving my fingers on my knees like he was doing. Every now and then he would look to see if I was paying attention and would give me a big toothy grin. I really enjoyed this time of evening with my father and Pops my grandfather. Ma joined us along with everyone else. She poured cold glasses of sweet homemade sassafras tea for us. We drank and talked quietly while listening to the piano and the crickets in the grass near the porch. I remember enjoying watching the full moon rising during the evening feeling so content and safe.

There were two other times my father became totally engrossed in his piano playing. He played the piano at our church every Sunday. He played before the preacher got started, to get the congregation wrapped securely within the Holy Spirit. It was a Pentecostal church so there was a lot of shouting, clapping, spirit dancing in the aisles, and people talking in tongues. I always stood beside the piano with my father shaking a tambourine and keeping up with him. The more he worked up the congregation, the more he seemed like he went into a trance. His whole body was animated including his head, fingers of course, but also his feet as he pumped the pedals. I could feel the vibrations coming up through the floor boards of the stage, and into my body. The entire atmosphere was infectiously contagious. It seemed that he infected everybody with his spirited music making. You could not be there without it touching you, moving you, energizing your whole beingness. It felt like we needed it.

By the time the preacher came out the entire church was virtuously spirited and unabashedly expressing it. There was a brief pause during which my father would strike some loud harmonious chords followed by shouts from the congregation, with exultations of amen, amen, glory, glory, praise God, and just shouts of joy over and over. The preacher in his elaborately detailed black robe, held up his hands with a white handkerchief in one, and looked out over his congregation nodding his head and making eye contact. This brief pause would end, and the preacher took over and raised the congregation to a new level of excitement and exclamation of the Holy Spirit. My father and I kept right up with him for hour after hour. My shirt was soaking wet and sticking to my back. The bench on which my father sat was wet in the shape of his buttocks. He wiped his forehead with the sleeve of his already wet white shirt never faltering, while sustaining the cadence with the preacher.

Sometimes I would look out at the congregation to see my family. They were always sitting on the same pew, the same aisle, and Pops was right next to the center aisle walk way that lead down the center of the church. They were all standing of course participating in the praise worship. Pops was very much into the praise and ceremony. He told me once it was important because it reminded him of our ancestors and the tribal ceremonies both Indian and African. For him it was a real connection to those ancient customs. He told me the most important thing for him and all of us was giving honor and recognition to the great creator in the sky. The creator from whence we all came and we all must and will return.

I could see him moving with his head tilted back, eyes closed and his lips moving. My cousins told me that he would speaks softly in the Choctaw language and sometimes he even shouted out some words especially when others were saying Praise God, Praise God. We all needed Pops and his guidance both in spiritual and everyday common-sense ways.

Pops just stopped breathing one day. That's what they said. He didn't die. He just stopped breathing and his heart ceased to beat. He was never sick, didn't take medicine other than what he mixed and brewed from herbs and plants he knew about in the woods. That day when he stopped breathing, his spirit went on, as he always said, to the Great Creator in the sky. People said it was just his time. The Creator wanted this good man back in the unseen spirit world.

The church was over flowing with people of all walks of life, for his going home services. They came from the city, the countryside, and those from the reservation were all dressed in their traditional garb. The church was completely full. Large crowds surrounded the outside of the church since there wasn't space inside. Ma asked about all the people, wondering how they all knew Pops Lakestone. He touched so many just by being himself. People felt the need to be present to honor him and pay respect for who he was as a person, a father, and a man of powerful wisdom.

My father was so pleased with the turn out and the special ceremony the Choctaws performed. He surprised me with how composed he was throughout everything. He didn't suffer in grief like I thought he would. Nothing at all like I did. I saw him go off to himself and stood in silence looking up into the sky for a short period. After that he took time to comfort and console everybody else. He made sure it was a happy homecoming for Adam "Pops" Lakestone.

Although my father didn't see himself living off the land forever. There were a lot of good times looking back and recalling things. We had hard times and struggles as well. My father had his mind set on becoming an accomplished jazz pianist. Of course, he took care of the family and provided, but still in the back of his mind he saw himself as a performer an entertainer. Just thinking about it I recall rolling on the floor with laughter and tears, hearing the story about the time the pastor of the church and my father ended up in the same place, and it wasn't in the Pentecostal church.

 Ma knew he was performing at this illegal night club in town on Saturdays. He got paid on the side a few bucks. It wasn't a whole lot. That wasn't the point. He was so enthralled with the fact that he was playing with a small jazz quartet as the lead pianist. Just how he played the piano on Sundays in church with such conviction and trance like animation, is how he attacked the keys on the piano at the club. Ma called it…. "that joint!" She went on and on about how dangerous it was, and what type of unsavory people went there. She talked about the gambling, drinking, and the drugs going on. She forbade me to even think about going there under the promise of what she would do to me if I did.

They called my father Stone at the joint. Short for Lakestone but meaning he was stone crazy when he sat down at the piano. One night during rehearsal the drummer was watching him and said, that man is stone crazy. The others burse into loud laughter and together said "Stone Crazy!" Stone stopped playing because he was laughing so hard himself. He had the same movements and theatrics as in church, but different music and message in the joint. However, he gave both audiences what they needed, what they wanted to feel. That's why they said Stone was a born professional. He took everything to another unexpected level when he performed.

Anyway, as the story goes one night my father was performing with the quartet at the joint. It was near the finale of a set to close the night. My father usually lead the group in a series of jazzed up arrangements popular with the crowd to close out. Stuff they liked to dance to.

Everybody jammed the floor to dance just when the bartender made the

last call announcement.

Suddenly, there was some commotion behind the stage curtains. My

father could hear loud bumping and things crashing. Then there was a

shrieking scream. Everyone stopped and looked at each other. Those on

the dance floor did the same. Suddenly a man ran out from the

backstage area followed by another man, and a screaming woman behind

the second man. The man ran so fast right up to the stage towards Stone.

It seemed like the whole scene was moving in slow motion. By the time

the man reached Stone he tripped and fell right at Stone's feet. Stone

looked down at the man in shock and amazement and said, "Pastor

Oliver?" Pastor Oliver from the Pentecostal Church looked back at Stone

and said, "is that you Lakestone?" The other man and woman tripped

over a table and were assisted out by the club's bouncer. Everybody in

the whole town heard about Pastor Oliver messing around with another

man's wife and got caught. Ma told the story many times and would

laugh so hard she cried but would end with a serious look telling us we

still better not ever, ever, go to the joint. The more she said don't, the

more we decided we had to.

****

Ahh shit! I got up early with the intention to get the day started and prepared for a good day. To start off on the right foot as they say. I spent too much time sitting here reminiscing about the past. Thinking about family and things that happened. I think I'm going to talk with Ma this weekend. She always likes going back and remembering. She has some good stories. I better get moving before Zena comes in and finds me like this. Ooop! Here she comes. Too late.

"Good morning Mar. Did you sleep? Or…!" "Come here and give me some suga babe. I know you slept girl! Snoring and slobbering as usual." "Marlon, you always accuse me of snoring, when you know I don't and you…." "Hah! Zena please you know."

"I know I sleep deeply that's all. Wow look what time it is. Aren't you going to work today it's already 7:15? Man! I'm going to be late too! Mar!" "Yeah I'm going…I just want to plunk out a few bars on my key board before I leave. Got a gig coming up."

"What! This morning? Now? I thought that you liked your job, and" "Come on Zena. Let's not go there please. Not this morning at least." "Yes, I'm still thinking about you last night and that dream or was it a nightmare. I wasn't going to bring it up. I don't want to go through all

23

that again Marlon. I really don't but." "Do we have to talk…?" "Yes Marlon, because you go into denial, then you get angry, and then depressed. What do you want me to do? How do you think I feel when…?" "Oh Zena. Stop please. I'm not one of your patients."

I should have been more careful and prepared knowing Zena was still thinking about last night. But, I messed up sitting here day dreaming or whatever dreaming it is I'm doing. She suddenly grabs her backpack, briefcase, and a stack of folders walking towards the door. I say aren't you going to say goodbye and give me a kiss at least. She stops turns around, walks over, and gives me a kiss on the forehead. I tell her I love her, and she continues out of the house and into her car. I hear the car start and then the tires squeaking on the driveway.

"Have a good day babe."

Here I am still in my pajama bottoms, sitting on the sofa with the electric key board in from of me. I run up and down the scales on the keys a couple of times. Waiting to let some rhythms surface hoping I come up with a new and catchy arrangement. My creative juices just won't start. I keep trying…nothing. So, I just start playing some Gershwin's Rhapsody in Blue to keep me in practice.

****

It's an old man. A very old man with a bald head, and a scruffy grey beard. He is lying in the middle of a bed in the fetal position. There is a rumpled once white sheet on the bed. The room is dark and drab. The bed is the only furniture in the gloomy room. There aren't even windows and nothing on the walls except one large, out of date, damaged, and stained Sears Roebuck calendar.

Suddenly, the old man changes position and turns on his side facing the opposite direction, but still in a fetal position. He is only wearing some dingy boxer shorts. Brown stains cover the original white color. A drop of water lands on the side of his face. It startles him. He turns again facing towards the wall, still in the fetal position. He draws his knees up closer to his chest. His ribs are quite noticeable as well as his boney legs and unusually large knee caps. Another drop of water hits his face. He startles again and quickly flips over on his back. He opens his murky cataract covered eyes, and his large toothless mouth. He appears to look through the cataracts up to see where the water is coming from. There is a large brown water stain where water has accumulated above the ceiling somehow. The ceiling stain is bulging from the water that has gathered there.

The drip, drip, drops from the ceiling becomes a continuous flow of water. It is landing on the old man's face and chest. He begins to choke and suddenly sits up on the edge of the bed with his boney legs hanging over the mattress. The water falling from the ceiling becomes a stream of water now. It fills the spot where the old man had been lying and fills the impression left by his body as a puddle. The man stands and shuffles across the room exiting and begins walking down a long hallway. The ceiling crashes with a loud blast as water cascades off the bed onto the floor and into the hall. The old man still struggles to walk down the hall. He is grasping his crotch as he needs to pee and can hardly hold it. He tries to speed up but can only shuffle along. The rushing water from the room is up to his knees with the unusually large caps. Finally, he reaches the toilet at the end of the hall. He pulls the cord on the light hanging from the ceiling. The sound of running water is evident. The bath tub is filled with dark churning water. The old man stands in front of the urinal. He pees on himself because the toilet is filled with thick dark oozing black liquid. The liquid slowly over flows forming globs that float on top of the water filling the bathroom. He turns around with a look of fear and anguish as urine runs down his legs and soaked shorts. Suddenly, the toilet explodes with water shooting up like a water spout.

The old man's lips begin to move. He opens his mouth wide, eyes are wide; and he shouts out something unintelligible. The old man looks down and water has gathered up around his soaked waist. He begins to shout over and over "Chickamaug! Chickamaug! CHICKAMAUG!"

"Ahh! I can't breathe. Oh God no. Stop! Please!"

I jumped up so fast I knock over the key board in front of me and walk rapidly in a small circle like I'm lost. The key board is upside down on the floor and a few keys are stuck and the sound coming out is so eerie. It's so bizarre. I've been dreaming again. I can't run away from it. I was just sitting here playing my key board. And now I wake up slumped back on the sofa, jump up like some crazy man....... "ZENA!"

I have a meeting with my boss Mr. Jackson this morning. I'm not looking forward to it, yet at the same time I do want to talk with him. If only he's in a good mood, which I doubt, like the atmosphere here in the lobby of the hotel.   It is December 1963 and Christmas decorations have been up way before Thanksgiving. I still can't get use to Christmas in LA. I remember the first Christmas here and I wore shorts in 70-degree weather or should I say heat since that is how it felt to me that day.

I really like my position as the Concierge in of all places the Hotel Biltmore. In this day and time in Los Angeles for a black man, that is unusual. I consider myself lucky and fortunate to have this job. I started off working in reservations. I could have just as well been hired as part of the kitchen staff. You know. But, an acquaintance of Zena's vouched for me to get in for the interview. I never met the person or her husband who is a power broker in LA. The wife participated in a support group for women, which Zena facilitated. Her husband pulled some strings and magically I had an interview with Mr. Jackson and eventually the reservation job. The interview was kind of uncertain at the end. It was my first experience up close with Mr. Jackson. I got to see his perpetual negative mood. I learned that he is actually a good man considering.

I held the reservation position for about three months and happened to be in the right place at the right time to land the Concierge job. That was truly a creation of the stars in my favor. Such a crazy day in the hotel when everything bad could happen and it did. Mr. Jackson looked and acted like he was spawned from hell that day.

There was this huge business conference going on and the hotel was completely occupied. It happened on the last day of the conference when it is always a mad house in the hotel. The lobby was full of people checking out all at the same time and new guest checking in. Every one of them needed something and had fifty questions each.

The actual Concierge was in a five-car accident on that curvy Pasadena freeway. His assistant and my friend Judy was in the hospital ready to deliver a baby. Great for her. Miserable for me. There wasn't the usual line of taxis outside the hotel entrance. The taxi union had declared a strike when negotiations fell through. I tell you, what could go wrong did, and what was generally a routine happening turned into the impossible.

Mr. Jackson approached me in the mists of all the madness. To my shock and surprise, he told me to take over as the Concierge and take care of everything in the hotel lobby. Did I say everything? I stood in shock with my mouth open and not moving. Mr. Jackson looked at me with a curious look and said well Marlon get to it. I said all right you got it. Wondering why those words came out of my mouth. But I snapped to attention and decided to first address the bulging gathering of hotel guests needing attention. They were very upset about the taxi situation. All of them had flights leaving LAX that morning. As they talked to each other the anger increased. It was the hotel's problem that they were going to miss their flights. I decided to address the largest group right in front of check-out first. The crowd was loud, demanding, and ready to have someone's head. There were six who needed to get to the airport within the hour. Four were headed for New York, and the other two were on a flight to London. Most of the others had flights that allowed sufficient time for them to arrive at LAX.

Judy was having her first baby, so she wasn't here but her special resources were. So, I tapped into them as best I could. I called her uncle in China Town. It took me a few minutes to get through the excitement he was shouting about Judy having a baby. Finally, he said oh yeah man what you need. Lucky for us China Town was just blocks away, and North of downtown LA. He sent over a fleet of his limos to carry all the hotel customers headed home to LAX and their flights.

Damn! I said I wanted to talk to Mr. Jackson this morning and here he comes. After all that chaos, I didn't have time to prepare myself. I'm sweaty, slightly rumpled and I feel a little out of sorts. But so, what. What's new?

"Good morning Mr. Jackson. Everything is under control and……." "Yes, yes, I see. Come with me Marlon. I need you. Hurry let's go where we can talk".

I stumbled a step following quickly behind Mr. Jackson, as I try to straighten my shirt and tie and shake this queasiness I feel in my stomach. We ended up behind a large partition on the other side of where the reservation staff welcomes new guest. I walked right into Mr. Jackson because he stopped so quickly, turning around and spoke right into my face, nose to nose. I can felt his hot stinky breath.

Hey Jackson. This is not how it was supposed to go. I wanted to say. I was supposed to take the lead and talk about...

Mr. Jackson was obviously upset, and breathing heavy, which made his halitosis worse. But all I could do was listen and take it in. It didn't take too many words to learn there was a big problem on the third floor in the main suite number 300A. Mr. Jackson got a call from security, who got a call from housekeeping, who got a call from a guest who reported a growing puddle of water in the hallway. Housekeeping had sent a maid

up to take carry of the mess. Mrs. Ruiz was the lead person for the

housekeeping team on that floor. Security reported that she was

hysterical, and they knew something was wrong, but they couldn't fully

understand her. She was so frightened and excited that she couldn't

remember enough English to explain what she saw in 300A.

"Malo, malo. Es muerto!"

"Marlon take care of this. Get up there and at all cost fix it. Make sure

that none of our guest become alarmed or frightened. And don't let the

staff panic. I could put someone else on this, but you are the man I need.

Report back to me and tell me what you need."

Before I could say anything, he pushed pass me and left just as quickly. I

saw him take the back elevator I assume to go to his office to meet with

the executive staff. I thought nothing I could have said or done would

change my position. No time to be afraid. So, get your ass up there

Marlon Lakestone.

By the time I walked off the elevator Bill and Tony accompanied me.

Two men from maintenance I could count on. They were dressed in

their green uniforms with shirt and matching pants. Bill, I have known

as long as I can remember. He serves on the church board with my mother and is a family friend. Despite his age Bill is still a fit man. Still bulky and strong. He wore his shirt outside his pants to give his belly a little room.

Tony has been with the hotel for many years and manages housekeeping and maintenance. He carries all his wisdom and knowledge on his face in each line and fissure. His big brown eyes are filled with compassion and understanding. He helped to calm down Mrs. Ruiz by speaking to her in her first language, Spanish. Just his presence and warmth settles things. He knows all the secrets about the hotel and its history. He showed me the ropes, and quick ways to get up and down, in and out of the building.

I assigned Bill and Tony to start cleaning detail for the water and mess in the hallway. More importantly I wanted them to present a calm presence in the hallway and not to let anyone near suite 300A. Not even staff. They were more like guards, but we didn't need guest to see security standing in the hall. This would obviously raise questions and possible alarm. But security was for sure involved. Just not visible at this point.

I walk slowly towards the end of the hall and suite 300A. I wished that I didn't have to hear that swish of the water, with each step that I take on the soaked carpet. So much water flowed under the door and down the hall. I'm surrounded by hundreds of rapid thoughts, with double the questions plaguing me. There is just one answer. Fix this and get back to normal. Normal, I ask myself, would be sitting at my key board right now. Mellowing out some Coltrane. Yeah!

I stop at the door with my hand nearly grasping the door knob and warn myself to be careful not to touch or disturb anything. I use the end of my suit coat to turn the knob. I've already called the police and they are on the way besides Zena's brother who works at LAPD in narcotics. I need his experience even if this isn't about drugs. Hopefully he will help me make this go away as quickly, quietly, and correctly as possible.

More water rushes out as I push the door to enter the room. It is clear. The water is coming from the bathroom. I see where the housekeeper who entered the suite dropped her clip board and a stack of towels that are soaked in a pile on the floor.

I hear water slowly running in the bathroom and push the door open for a full view. I see a woman floating in the bathtub her head submerged under the water. She is fully clothed in all white. On the vanity is an obvious suicide note. No, it is a long suicide letter. Without picking it up, I quickly scan the letter. It's written to Daddy, and one line strikes me hard.

"Look at me daddy. You see me. I AM your daughter".

 There appears to be scattered family photos on the vanity as well. Some of the photos float on the surface in the bathtub with her. The photos are of children, adults, and family events. They all show happy times. I take a long look at the woman. Her face is peaceful, but her once pink skin is dull and graying in color. Her seemingly hazel eyes look murky. Her long blonde hair floats around her beautiful face like a frame. I think she should have been loved. Why not? I see a small bubble escape from her nostril, like it was the final sign. Finality is a bitch.

"Es muerto".

That dizzy, queasy feeling is trying to creep up on me again. Enough. I gotta get out of here. I know what comes next. I use a hand towel to turn off the water running into the tub. I know I shouldn't leave my finger prints here. I leave with some resolve.

I retrace my tracks with the same swishing sound walking out of the suite. This time thoughts of sadness and remorse. Thoughts of family. My family. I want to talk to Ma. I haven't seen her or spoken with her in a while. It will be good for me and Zena.

Man! I thought I was going to be able to catch a break after all of that. But here I am on the way to Mr. Jackson's office. I'm sure he wants to bust my balls about something I did wrong. I'm sure of that. What else could it be? I stop at the door, take a deep breath, and knock as I slowly open the door. He is sitting at his desk of course, but he is smiling at me as I enter.

"Marlon my man! Come on in. Have a seat. Take a load off."

Am I dreaming? I can't believe what I'm hearing. Mr. Jackson is smiling and in a good mood. What's up with this? Some weird way to say it ain't working and just fire me. I slowly ease the chair back facing him and sit with apprehension. He suddenly gets out of his chair, walks quickly around the desk, and takes the other chair right next to me. It is so foreign to see him smiling. I can see teeth I didn't know he had. He places his hand on my arm in a comforting way. This man has never touched me. I've never notice how big Mr. Jackson is being this close to him. His hands are big, and I see purple brown liver spots on them. He must be close to 60 but looks younger. My mother would call the way he is dressed as perspicuity. His suit is a navy-blue pin stripped. The crispy light blue button downed shirt is complimented with a cobalt blue tie with specks of gold. The pocket of the suit jacket has a cloth patch of gold and blue. His wing tip burgundy shoes have a military shine. He has strong facial features with a square jaw topped off with salt and pepper hair cut in a buzz. He is all put together.

"Thank you, Marlon. You handled that so well. I appreciate everything you did. I could have asked George in security, but he doesn't have the finesse like you do man. So, tell me about it. How'd it go?"

I'm confused. What is he talking about. I really don't understand where all this happiness about what happened is coming from. I really don't know what to say, but I can't sit here looking stupid. I'm right here in this man's office. It's what I wished for this morning. And now I'm searching for what to say.

"Tell me again. What was that fool's name? I'm not that out of touch. I might be a little old, but I would know a star with top billing. You know what I mean?"

The more he talks the more I'm not understanding a damn thing about what he is saying. He said star. He is asking about some man he thinks I had some contact with, or I don't know what. This is getting worse. This is fucking with me right now.

"Mr. Jackson. Are you talking about what happened up in 300A? I'm sorry for asking you that, but" "What are you apologizing about Marlon. You took the bull by the horns and kicked ass. I saw Bill and Tony. They told me about some chicks up there too. That's how those entertainment people do their thing." "Mr. Jackson. I'm sorry but are you talking about the woman in the bathtub? And you sound like you heard about a group of people being up there?"

"Nobody was in the bathtub. Someone must have been planning to take a bath or whatever. One of them left the water running. Mrs. Ruiz saw the water when she opened the door and found that jerk with three women. They were knocked out I guess from drugs and alcohol. Who knows what? They were all naked man. There were all kinds of trash, and booze all over the place in that suite. The furniture was moved and tossed around the room like they didn't care. Half eaten food and food containers were spread about the room, even in the bathroom. Were they that hungry?"

"You got them out with your contacts at LAPD. That's what I liked the most. It was done so discretely, so as not to put us in a bad spot with the news. Our house guess didn't even have a clue. I still can't think of that assholes name. He was performing in a hugh concert at the Shrine

Auditorium. He was one of the lead up performers for the main act. I think it was Eric Clapton who had top billing. That fool sure was the main act here at the Biltmore, but he flopped."

"Look Mr. Jackson, I…" "Oh, for Christ sake Marlon quite trying to down play this thing. You did what I asked you and I appreciate it. You just don't know how much. Now I have to leave. I got stuff to do with the finance director. Now make yourself a drink. The liquor is over there. Oh yes. I added some fat to your Christmas bonus as my appreciation Mr. Lakestone."

What just happened? What is going on with me? Am I cracking up? This isn't real. What the… I feel better having my break and drink down hear in the lounge. I feel more in touch with these people eating their lunch. This vodka tonic is hitting the spot even though I asked the bartender to only pour in half the vodka and all the tonic.

I know I went to the third floor. I know I saw and talked to Bill and Tony. Hey, I shook hands with both. How much more real is that. Shit my shoes are still soggy from walking in that damn water. WATER! Yeah, damn straight there was water. That's for sure. Got you there Mr. Jackson. Even you said water. Mrs. Ruiz bless her sweet heart said water.

Seems like when I felt dizzy… Oh shit. Was I dreaming or in some dream trance….

Oh Lord……. Help me. Make this go away.

"Sorry Mr. Marlon. I didn't quite hear you. You want your drink refreshed?" "Hey Joey. Hard day. I guess I was mumbling to myself. Do me a favor. Take Harvey over at the piano whatever he is drinking. Put it on my tab. Thanks. I guess I will have another of the same. Half the vodka."

Am I losing it? Am I losing control? This stuff happened, and it seems like I didn't even know it, or have control over it or me. Please……

The lunch crowd has clear out of the lounge. It will be quiet until Happy Hour. I need to talk and make sense with another person. It will be cool to catch up with Harvey and chat with him at his piano.

"Marlon! Thanks for the drink. Right on time man. What you up to brother?" "Hey Harvey. I'm doing okay. How about you?" "You must be having a pretty rotten day man. What you need is to come down to the old Dunbar Hotel and jam with us one night. Central Ave is coming back. Since they have been revitalizing the Dunbar and the businesses around it. Central Ave is becoming a good place to go and enjoy some good jazz in Los Angeles like it was back in the day.”

“You don't look good Marlon. I was watching you from over here. You had your head hanging down and slumped over your drink, and I even thought you might have been talking to yourself. That ain't you.” “Well Harvey you are right. It has been a messed up day. Some junky musician had an after party here at the hotel after performing at the Shrine Auditorium. They trashed the place and let the bathtub over flow and run out into the hallway. I took care of it, but it drained me. I'll be back to myself when I get some good sleep. But yeah. I'm gonna do that. I really want to have a little jam session with y'all. I'm happy to hear about the Dunbar.”

“Hey man. Take care of yourself. Get some rest and let me see you down at the Dunbar.” “You got it Harvey. For sure man.”

If only he knew how much my soul needs to be playing and making music right now. I don't need or want all of this. Dealing with other people's problems and having to work with a man who is always angry. He shocked me when he was so nice. He smiled and shook my hand. Was that real? Who knows? Who knows at all what was today? Do I?

Getting off early and leaving the hotel is so good. It was another unexpected gift from Mr. Jackson. He fooled me again about his character. I decided to do some shopping. Central Market is the largest place to buy groceries and meat in the downtown area. There is a variety of other goods and services available there too.

I walked over to Central Market from the hotel. Thought about what to cook for Zena tonight. Something good and something we haven't had in a while. After walking up and down the aisles decided on two specialty cut steaks, two big potatoes to bake, some fresh spinach to cream, a bunch of mushrooms to sauté, salad greens, and a good bottle of wine. Not too creative, but this is going to be good and Zena will enjoy not having to throw something together for dinner. She'll be blown away to walk in, see the table already set, and smell some delicious food cooking. I will even clip some roses from the yard for the table.

Of course, she was surprised, and saying she enjoyed it would be an understatement. While we savored my culinary skills, I took this time to tell her about my day. She was just as shocked when I told her about Mr. Jackson calling me to his office and described the unbelievable way he approached me with kindness. I thought she would be amazed when I described the room and what happened in the hotel suite. She just laughed. When I told her about the water flowing from the bathtub and how Ms. Ruiz found it running under the door, her eyes got wide, and she laughed again. Her only comment was, "In the Biltmore? Come on Mar. You gotta be making this up."

I assured her I wasn't. I got quiet after that and focused on my steak. She took a fork full of spinach and just looked at me waiting for me to speak again. I kept chewing, but finally swallowed and looked up at her.

"Zena may I tell you something that has bothered me? I haven't ever talked to anyone else about this before." "Okay Mar…… What is it?" "You know how I told you about the over flowing bathtub? Well when I walked up to it and looked down into it……. It reminded me of something back when I was maybe 13 or 14."

I stopped and found myself starring off again.

"Go on Mar. I'm listening.… What was it? Did somebody hurt you or something?" "No, no.… I don't really know.… It reminded me of when I was baptized in church. It was like when we were in a class with the pastor. He presented the seriousness of being baptized and what it represented for us spiritually. I accepted everything about it as being very important. I looked forward to that day in church when it would happen. One Sunday after service, I stood by myself just looking at the baptismal pool and the water in it. I thought that the water had to be holy. The night before, I couldn't sleep thinking about it. I kept praying over and over asking Jesus to help me with it."

"Aaaw that's so cute Mar." "I'm being serious Zena."

I drifted off and didn't say anything again staring at a candle flame flickering on the table.

"I wanted to feel something…... When I came up out of the water I wanted to feel something. I wanted to feel different. My eyes were open, and I could see the water wash over me as I felt them pulling me up out of the water……. Nothing was there. No feeling that was different."

"Oooh Mar baby. Did you talk to the pastor about it?" "No. I didn't tell anyone or ask anyone about it. I thought……. something was wrong with me and if I talked about it everybody would know." "Know what Marlon?" "Know that it didn't happen, so something must have been wrong with me. I was the same when I came up out of the water. The water was supposed to change me."

"Marlon, you were young and impressionable then. You were sensitive too. Maybe your expectations were……." "Thanks for listening Zena. I don't want to talk about it anymore. It's taking me down and I don't want to feel down tonight. This was supposed to be a pleasant night for us." "OK Mar I'll have some more wine, and oh yes. What did you make for dessert monsieur chef?" "Can't you smell it?" "No, I can't smell anything. Is it in the oven?"

"Come on Zena. Sniff your nose like this…. Smell it yet?" "Nooo." "It's me. Good to lick the icing off me. Eat me up. Zena, I want to take one of those erotic showers with you. I want you to suds me all up with that good smelling soap. And then I will suds you up with my body until…… You know what I'm talking about. Just get busy with each other. Make each other feel sooo good. I want you woman." "Can I get on top Mar?" "Oh yes. You so nasty woman. Just so I can kiss that spot of yours?" "Can I put my mouth all over yours? I'm getting wet right now."

Zena got up, walked over to me, and cuddled in my lap. We kissed passionately, caressed each other, and roamed over each other's bodies. That lasted for a few minutes and we walked to the shower, stripping off our clothing as we went. I let her beat me getting undress. She went to the shower and I got some candles and lit them around in the bedroom. I let my sensitive romantic side take over and guide me towards what we both needed and wanted.

How do I describe what took place in our bed? How fortunate that she likes sex just as much as I do. Look at her. Already sleep. Usually I doze off first. Just goes to show she puts as much into it as I do. None of that male selfishness. Get off and forget about her. We complement each other. She drives me to the edge where I'm right at release and she draws me back just in time and keeps the rhythm on hit. And I do the same with her. We may both go to the edge 2 or 3 times each. It's a lot of hot sex, but it is deeper passionate love making than anything. Climaxing for us is so powerful. Most times we can achieve it simultaneously. It just happened that we are this way. Mutually committed to total pleasure for each other. I think it is funny sometimes how she talks dirty. I must dig deep to come up with something to say that tops her nasty little comments. It so funny. She is Ms. Sophisticated Social Worker during the day. I love it and wouldn't change it at all. Damn. I'm hard again and she is asleep…. Nope. Really, I'm worn out. Sleep is just a nod away.

The steep stairway is dark and ominous looking. The stairs are covered with worn down raggedy once plush blood red carpet. The steep journey on the history laden stairs up looks labored. Once at the top the lighting is brighter. It's a long hallway, almost tunnel like. The walls are covered with fading red faux velveteen. The walls show patterns of large trees without leaves. Numerous blotched spots hide the original richness. Lining the hallway walls are large elaborate gold sconces. The light bulbs in the sconces are from another era. Even more elaborate are the high back chairs upholstered in red velvet. The heavily craved arms and legs are covered in gold leaf. On either side of the large chairs are floor to ceiling beveled mirrors. Further down the hall is an extremely large chandelier. It's covered with dangling crystal prisms. A strange sound, somewhat vibrating, somewhat rumble begins. Or it was always there but it's more noticeable now. Two very large doors at the end of the hallway appear. Each door has a huge gold handle surrounded by intricate carvings. Water is flowing under the doors and into the hallway. Suddenly, the vibrating rumble is extremely loud. The chandelier is shaking, and the dangling crystal prisms are swinging about causing a high-pitched clinking sound. The water has become a torrent flood splashing high up the sides of the wall. The hallway quickly fills with the thrashing water. The red chairs are bobbing about in the sudden flooded hallway. Portions of the red faux velveteen wall covering is peeling off. It looks like gooey layers of dirt filled vomit. It flows down into the rapidly rising foul looking water. Finally, the large doors burst open as the horrid water flows down the hallway. The waves tumble over and over. All the high back chairs tumble and cascade down the stairs. The water reaches the sconces while sparks fly, and the old light bulbs explode. The rumbling sound is much louder and threatening. Without warning a huge black lacquered grand piano hits the frame of the doors. The doors collapse as the piano rapidly crashes forward from the force of the water. The vibrating keys of the piano strike an oddly eerie tune. The piano bounces off the sides of the wall crashing and breaking the mirrors from one side of the hall to the other. Predictably the piano lumbers over the pinnacle of the steep stairs. It topples over and over itself, keys striking a painful tune of doom. The water has subsided. There is just a trickle of water where a soggy page of sheet music flows effortless down the stairs and stops at the last soggy step.

I find myself in the dark looking in the bathroom mirror. I questioned myself, asking if I have lost it. Crazy. I'm glad this time that I didn't jerk sitting up in bed choking or gasping. Zena doesn't know this time. That leaves me… I don't either…. I must stop lying to myself. Denial doesn't work and for sure doesn't fix anything. More than anything it makes things worse. I hate lying to Zena. But my motive is to protect her. I don't want to take her there again. No… and I won't. I just need……

"Mar. Hey Mar, are you up already? Why are you in there in the dark?"

"Yes, I'm up already. You know how I sit on the toilet in the dark to just think. Not about anything serious. You know I just sit here. I need a shower now."

It was good that she wasn't thinking that something was wrong. Or had an opportunity to catch me startling out of a dream in a panic state again! I finished a quick shower and went back into the bedroom and the bed where she was just relaxing while thumbing through a magazine. I snuggle up to her.

"Good morning Mrs. Lakestone. I love you woman." "Uum, Marlon you smell good." "Wow! And you stink. Where did you sleep last night?" "Okay you. Let me go. I'm going to get ready for work." "Wait, wait. I forgot to tell you something last night. Mr. Jackson gave me the day off, and I'm going over to Ma's to spend the day with her. I haven't talked with her in days." "Oh Mar. I want to go too. But I have a big meeting today." "I know you do babe. How about we both go back this weekend and have dinner with her."

*****

What would make the land contemplate existing in a pedestrian state?

How could this rich, rich, soil forego its fertile history to even approach a

dormant decay. So previously fruitful and abundant. So willing to spread

and release its abundance and prosperity freely. Old Mother Earth

appeals to its subservient rich soil to be thy own magnificent boldness.

Grow. Produce. Reproduce. Multiple again.

The Mississippi spring arrives on times. However, in Holmes

Mississippi it doesn't look like the rebirth of all given life. It doesn't feel

like an embrace given by the magnificent Divine upon the Earth for

fruitful rejuvenation. The sky is high with flattened clouds and presents

a depressing gray. While the land is degraded and putridly dry.

"Pops has some land."

The land that was Pop's pride and reason for living, no longer has the will

to grow, to produce, to reproduce. The acres, and acres of crops have

descended into disheartened impotence. Even the cotton and sugar cane

51

crops once so lucrative are in a state of failure. No longer a vision of rolling soft waves of livelihood.

In Holmes, the whole town knew about Adam Lakestone's cotton crop. He matched many of the white farmers in cultivating and harvesting a bumper season of sugar cane. This could only happen in Holmes Mississippi. A Choctaw man successfully cultivating a yearly crop of cotton and sugar cane.

The course began in the spring with the planting. Pops would nurture, watch, and nourish his fields of white gold. He would sit back and watch the cotton plants develop. He would walk down the long furrows of cane stalks and know his success. He recognized signals as the cotton plants grew. He especially relished seeing the plants flower. First the buds blossomed into a creamy white flower, followed by a yellow color, which turned pink. The final phase was when the pink flower turned red. This signaled the end and the shriveling, and withering of the flower, before it fell to the ground. How depressing not to see this colorful symphony played out in the life of a cotton bud. Unless you were close to the land like Pops was. You would not have known that the cotton plant could be so exciting. This same plant that contributed to so much pain, misery, and inhumane regard for the lives of so many black men, women, and children. This soil here no longer rejoiced when its cotton plant did not underwrite this inhumanity in a living tragedy.

No, no. The soil, the land, no longer felt the presence of Adam Lakestone walking upon it. His footsteps were so comforting, and nurturing to the land. When his naked hands dug down deep into the rich soil, there was complete harmonious motivation to reproduce in a springtime climatic birth, rebirth.

"Pops just stopped breathing. He didn't die. He just stopped breathing."

The land knew not how to interpret his disappearance, it just knew he, Adam Lakestone, was not there any longer. This springtime, the land is not breathing as it once did with such virility. The virility of its absent seed.

"Something happened to the water in the stream."

Pops had an early warning about the water in the stream. A harassing premonition overwhelmed him. He could only speculate that someone, something was polluting the stream water. This springtime the stream water doesn't flow any longer. It appears it is a struggle just to wet the deep fissures of its once vibrant past. A vitality that sustained and prolonged the vigor of the land.

This springtime there is barely a trickle of enthusiastic water to harmonize with the land. The enthusiasm does not exist any longer. Nearly dry, there is no sound of it rushing and swirling around rocks and boulders in the once swiftly moving cool pure forceful waves.

The premonition was not as feared. It was tremendously more ominous and debilitating. And this springtime confirms it. The source was with the Black River, which is the natural life giver of this stream. The stream just a minor fingerling of the Big Black, became impotent when the TVA, better known as the Tennessee Valley Authority constructed a dam. Prosperous reservoirs and large lakes were the results of the dam. The lifeless stream was the land's result, and Pop's premonition comes as factual. So depressingly devastating for the land.

Time before the dam, people of the land remembered when it rained for an entire winter. When it started everyone just thought that it was the familiar cyclical rain. That which arises ever winter to soak the land on behalf of spring and planting season. It was expected. It was due and on time. But the people of the land began to take notice that this rain time was different. Different in the sense that there was no stopping. No pause between down pours or days. Different in the sense that it was on-going, continuous, unremitting. At night, they retired to bed hearing it pound the roofs of their homes. They awoke alarmed that it was still coming forth. No loss in intensity.

People started making predictions about when it would stop. Others made speculations about its cause, its origin. The elders said that it was from the spirits. Spirits that had become displeased with how the land was being treated. How the land was not being properly cared for. Concern turned to fear, and fear lead to repeated prayers and offerings. Unvarying episodes of depression and slumped moods. Nerves were on edge and agitation was easily triggered.

"Oh Lord, God almighty. Let it stop. We honor and obey you Lord. Praise God. Praise God."

Nothing but nothing influenced the elements and the rain. It was raining continuously for weeks into more weeks. Regular customs changed. The temperament of the folks changed. A deep sense of gray dreary smothering gloom fell upon everything and everybody. Everyone felt it and tried to compensate for it. Families cloistered in their homes trying to deny their deepest fears. Only the children carried on as usual but protested not being able to romp outside as usual. Even the livestock looked dejected huddled up in the barns, stables, and lean-tos. Disoriented roosters did not crow while the unfamiliar ominous sky prevailed over the entirety.

The land could not absorb the amount of water sinking in to it. Without warning the once heavy rain turned into wind driven, nearly horizontal sheets of water. The winds howled, and intermittent thunder shook everything to the foundation. It reminded them of the spring tornadoes. But this was winter time. Not a time for a tornado. Things weren't as routine, so anything transpired. The fear turned into strangled trepidation. How do you grip your fear when you are powerless, helpless, with nowhere to turn for security or support?

"Oh glory, glory! We praise you Lord almighty. Let thy grace wash over us."

Day and night nearly looked the same. Some avoided looking out the windows. While others looked out and discovered the expected. The inevitable. Water gathering in pools that rapidly increased to ponds, and then menacing lagoons.

The fear manifested. The inevitable realization that another monstrous flood was upon the land. Even the ancient Indian mounds constructed by indigenous tribes to fortify the land from destructive flooding could not save this occasion, this season. The land of course remembered the legendary flooding and so did its dwellers. Such destruction cannot be forgotten. Etched in memories.

The flood waters recognized the familiar paths leading to the unification with the swamps. The thick lush Mississippi swamps of Cypress forest. With this flood, the swamp reversed its character of still stagnation, into a crusade pent up on utter destruction. Its sounding wake-up is quickened and enormously profound. The rapid response encompasses the entirety of the land, the streams, and the swamps. It was a swiftly moving destructive body of flooding water. Consuming everything in its constantly changing digestive path.

The flood waters revealed the secrets of the Cypress forest. The secret, oft hidden lives of native Black Bears, and Whitetail Deer for example. Bears that didn't flee soon enough, cling high in the branches of Cypress trees where they had never ventured to seek refuse. Deer attempting to swim to safety in the surging rapids of black angry churning water. Their fate doomed. All types of wildlife like raccoons and opossum seek safety from the flood. The elusive treacherous alligators and venomous water moccasins dangerously transverses and tread precariously near trees, swamp grasses, and other debris caught in the flood. Nothing is the same. Nothing is the same, and nothing is predictable. The only normal view is of flocks of pelicans, egrets, and cormorants flying to safer waters and land possibly far south to the gulf areas.

The flood knows its victims and does not hesitated to ruthlessly victimize the fullness within and around its course. Human victims floating in the rapids clinging to tree branches. Even on top of their homes, from which the waters sucked out all their precious possessions. Including dead family members. Further victimization and pain so indescribable. Who could even look at the human bodies floating lifelessly while being pummeled by boulders, trees, and all kinds of dense debris in the torrents of turbulent waves. The overwhelming crux of powerlessness. Manifested seeing only the arms of a parent holding up a small mud caked child. The child choking on the water washing across its face. Eyes wide and filled with fear.

"God have mercy."

A gathering of fortunate survivors viewed the desolation from a hill high enough to escape the enveloping rampage. Nearly everyone knew someone who drowned in the flood. Knew someone who had lost everything. All things holding meaning to them. Even those who had very little to call possessions felt the loss.

The human spirit motivates us to pursue ways to rescue, protect, and benefit others just like us as human beings. Something so destructive as a flood, killing, and ravaging lives evokes the spirit. Succeeding the flood this was the response. People were rescued out of the water, from places where they were trapped. The rain stopped, and the water stood still all around them. People found in the most amazing places where the water caused them to be in such precarious places. Like the mother and child clinging to an iron cross up high on a church steeple. The flood water laps at the eaves of the church roof. The mother waving frantically while the child appears to have died. The mother tied her child to the cross with strips of cloth torn from her ragged garments. So daunting to see. So peculiar a question. How did they end up there?

Flood water seen as far as the eye can see in every direction. The massive flood that gulped up over a million acres of Mississippi did not decide who would survive or who would die. It victimized the totality when it raped the levees with its black ocean. Inundating the lives of all of Mississippi's peoples. Yes, the human spirit was motivated to respond. To rescue those who were left. And there were still many. Many so numbed by the natural catastrophe that they walked aimlessly not knowing where to go, or what to do. They were broken down to the boundaries of mortality.

Was it strange that some rescued victims were ushered into places of respite, while others because of the color of their skin were herded into concentration like camps. African people of the time called colored, and the indigenous Indian people were forced into fenced areas with very little shelter and a scarcity of food. Most striking was the forces that guarded them with guns. How bizarre that they already lead difficult fringed lives and survived a natural catastrophe to find themselves in a greater misery driven by segregation. Life in the segregated camps was worse than the flood itself. This aftermath, another blow of destruction, washing away the pure dignity of life, with degradation lower than the silt of the flood.

The aftermath of the flood changed the land, and to a greater sense, changed the people of the land. People, specifically colored people back then, began to leave and migrate up North. It had been going on for some time as far back as World War I. The Great Migration is what it was called. It was going on before this massive flood in Mississippi. Life sounded better up North to escape Jim Crow and widespread lynching in the cotton states of the South. Those who left their families and homes and survived the hardship of the migration trail sent messages and letters back to towns and farms where they still had family and friends. They pleaded with their families to come too. Move up North.

Chicago was touted to be a better place with opportunities. A virtual promise land. Large numbers of people from the South migrated to Chicago, including from Pops Lakestone's family. This would have been so difficult for him had he still been alive. Pops would have strongly protested and preached how this was not of their ways. How could they think of leaving the land? Who would turn their backs on this land? Who would not carry on what Adam Pops Lakestone Sr. had spent his life creating and nurturing, for some place called Chicago.

The Second Day

Life is a bitch, and if it's not one damn thing, it's going to be something else... You don't let that stop you.

Count Bessie

I have mixed feelings about going to talk with Ma. It has been a while and that is all my fault. I know I need to. She has always grounded me when I most needed it. Right now, I really desire it considering all the bizarre stuff that has been happening with me. Still, I'm kind of hesitant about questions I want to ask, and things that might be creeping up from the past. I always do this. Stress myself out ruminating on everything forwards and backwards before I talk with Ma. It's all me. Has nothing to do with her. I've been here before dreading it, but in the end the comfort is mine. And then I feel foolish for beating myself up over pointless worry. Yet these dreams are becoming discomforting to me.

My mother, Elizabeth Lakestone better known as Lizzie, because that's what my dad affectionately called her, is my example of a life lived well. She left the Pentecostal Church when the family moved to Los Angeles years ago. She became a Practitioner in the Fountain of Life Religious Science Church. Church people had an adoring name for her. She became Mother Lizzie in her church and elsewhere. She stands about five feet, with maybe an inch more, as this short stout mighty pack of wisdom and compassion. She is firm with her beliefs and always projects her point with confidence and finesse even when she faces opposing positions. Her secret advantage is that infectious smile that radiates from her eyes. Her cinnamon brown eyes with the gray-blue ring around them from age, looks inside and holds you with warmth and empathy. Her smooth velvety face is framed by her full head of curly silvery hair. When I was a little boy she would ask me to brush her hair. Not because she was getting dress to go somewhere, but because she liked it and so did I. I didn't know what I was doing, so I just vigorously brush all her hair back. It was a comforting time for both of us. We didn't even talk. Sometimes she would hum softly, but that was it. I always got an invigorating hug afterwards. I forgot to tell you how much she issues out hugs. The hair brushing reminds me now of how she meditates. Our little hair brushing ritual was somewhat like meditation. After joining the Religious Science church, she really took on mindful meditation. It is a routine for her to meditate no less than twice per day. She enjoys it. It is her anchor in life, along with what she calls her power prayers. Her house smells like incense she burns when she meditates or prays. I guess it shows how much she does them both, because the pleasant aroma lingers all the time. It is not a harsh aroma but offers a peaceful and calming atmosphere.

Ma was born in Tupelo Mississippi, which is not that far from Holmes where I was raised by her and my father. Today she spends a lot of time in her yard like we all did in Holmes where the land dictated everything. Pops taught her about the earth and crops. She still maintains a plot of ground behind her house where she has a variety of vegetables growing. From collards to zucchinis. She keeps Pops close to her this way. Parts of the inside of here home looks like a jungle with all the house plants that she grows. We will probably sit on her wooden bench right next to the vegetable garden. It is underneath a fichus tree with a wind chime hanging in it. The space is Ma's peaceful and quiet place to read, converse, or just meditate. That wooden bench is weather worn but very sturdy in age, just like Ma.

Lizzie is retired from employment, but she has a full-time job devoting herself to life and others. She spends all day Sunday at church from the time she leads sunrise meditation, until after hospitality duties following the last congregation service at 1:00 P.M. Seems like her service to others never ends. I particularly remember her involvement with a young mother diagnosis with incurable brain cancer. Their relationship began when Lizzie was on duty in the prayer room when the young woman asked Ma to pray with her. Ma told me it was the most challenging practitioner work she had done. Her power prayer had to be just as strong for the young mother as it was for Ma. She needed to prepare herself as the relationship got deeper each time they had a session. The young mother had so much confidence in Ma and requested that my mother join her in her preparation for the end of her life. The diagnosis came early enough that hospitalization wasn't required at first. The type of cancer grew slow and quiet. Symptoms took time to appear and could change suddenly.

They talked about how and when to tell the young mother's children. She was the mother of two children. An eight year old daughter and a twelve year old son. Her husband was aware of the full details, but he wasn't providing the strength that she needed. He obviously needed support himself.

The young mother met Ma at church during the afternoon on week days when it was less busy. They became very close and trusting of each other. It was an extraordinary relationship founded in deep spiritual faith and beliefs. There were periods when the young mother became overwhelmed with debilitating depression. This happened when she thought about her children. It was difficult for her to think about the activities she would miss in their lives. Although it was not Ma's normal habit as a practitioner, she invited this young white mother to her home. My mother always shared her garden with friends and sometimes people she had just met for the first time. She prayed about it and decided that she could approach the depression in the garden. She was right. They met there every week. Sometimes they talked, while other times they worked together in the garden. I know Ma was humming softly the whole time they pulled bothersome weeds or used the hoes to till the rich soil. Of course, the old graying bench is where they held their discussions and prayed with power. At the close of visits, the young mother initiated a warm and sincere hug. She acquired Ma's habit of course. Neither of them felt uncomfortable when the hugging felt longer on some days.

Over the course of months, a plan of action was finalized to handle all aspects of what was likely to happen as well as the unforeseen, which they dreaded most. The young mother wanted to finalize planning with her doctor as much as possible. She invited Ma to go with her to her doctor appointments. She told Ma that sometimes she didn't remember everything the doctor said. She also worried that she wouldn't remember everything she want to ask or say to her doctor. Ma became her coach during these visits and the doctor appreciated her presence. The doctor thought that explaining symptoms was going to be tough. She was surprised when the young mother and Ma made light of the symptoms. They had already done some research on brain cancer symptoms. It was decided that they wouldn't give certain words like nausea and fatigue, power over their actions, and feelings. During meditation sessions, they visualized the symptom terms melting like candle wax. The doctor smiled hearing about their approached and teasingly asked Mother Lizzie if she wanted a job. She was thankful but wanted the young mother to really be prepared and gave her some pamphlets to take with her.

I don't remember how long it was after the doctor appointments, but things changed suddenly. Ma told me about the Sunday the ushers found her in church and told her that someone was outside the church insisting that she had to see Mother Lizzie. Ma hurried out. She didn't even have to think about it. She knew it was her. The young mother with brain cancer. Ma saw her sitting on the foundation of the beautiful water fountain in front of the church. The fountain with its multiple jets shooting streams of water high into the air and cascading down in rhythmic claps into the water normally would be the perfect backdrop for many occasions. Not this occasion with a foregone dire conclusion. Ma approached her, and without words, they grabbed each other immediately. The young mother tried to talk behind her tears but was having difficulty. Not because she was emotional and crying, but because something was wrong with her speech. She said her head was splitting and she could hardly stand the pressing pain. That night she had a massive stroke and was hospitalized. Two days later she succumbed to the evil tumor in her brain that grew uncontrolled. Mother Lizzie was in the hospital room along with the young mother's husband. The husband insisted, with the support of her doctor, that Mother Lizzie be allowed in the room since she was not a family member. Under different standards, she was actually.

Our family house is where my mother still lives after we moved. We left Chicago for Los Angeles. Moving to Los Angeles was another leg of the Great Migration. The migration of African Americans from the South lasted into the 70's. This migration was the movement of over six million rural black folks from the deep segregated south. They moved in groups, families and as individuals. They were seeking better lives and opportunity in cities like New York, Chicago, St. Louis, and Detroit. Most of the migrants from Mississippi ended up in Chicago. It wasn't uncommon for some of the northern industries to assist the people seeking better employment opportunities. These industries included railroad companies, meatpacking, and stockyard companies. In some cases, they paid for relocation and resettlement needs for the displaced.

The Chicago Defender, a newspaper owned and operated by an African American was where most people in the South, got their information about moving up north. The Chicago Defender kept people informed about the whole concept of migrating and provided helpful tips about what to expect. My father seemed to dream as he looked at pictures of people who had left Chicago. Coming from the peaceful rural area of Holmes Mississippi even with all the Jim Crow powers, Chicago provided opportunities, but it was very depressing where we had to live. It was not our own like we were used to. We all pooled our resources, which helped us survive and progress. But living in crowded conditions spurred on tension, disagreements, and didn't very often allow privacy or respite.

The migration created connection trails that beckoned others to follow. One family member moved, then sent back letters and later money so another family member or friend could follow too. Many times, the entire family could not move at once. Houses, apartments, and rooms were shared, just so they made it to Chicago. Their goal was to somehow have their own place no matter how long it would take. Their own little piece of freedom. Sadly, Chicago was not so free. All the migrants were forced to live in segregation mostly on the Southside of Chicago. It was still better that the Jim Crow segregated South.

In our case it was cousin Ida Mae that migrated first. She moved in with her uncle who lived in the housing projects where she shared the living room floor for sleep with three other family members. She worked long and hard to get her own place even though it was just two rooms. It was more than a year, before her husband and two children boarded a train to be with her and have their family together again. Being separated was tremendously difficult for the family, but the knowledge that they were going to be together again was heartwarming and exciting at the same time. The strength of family germinated the motivation to withstand demanding obstacles.

Her husband learned how to slaughter livestock from Pops Lakestone back in Holmes. With this knowledge, he was so lucky to land a job with a large meat packing plant in Chicago. That was the start of our migration trail when my father was invited to come too. He was assured that he could get work at the same packing plant. Ma was very reluctant at first, but finally joined Adam Lakestone Jr's quest for a better life in some place called Chicago.

I heard about what it took to get us ready to leave the land we all so

loved. The land that Pops taught us to appreciate and honor. My father

wouldn't talk about it, even though everyone was so supportive, it was

obvious he was hurting inside. Ma let flow enough tears for all of us. I'm

sure her tears that hit the earth went straight to Pops' spirit.

Ma told me her idea was to secure everything in our house and instantly

transport it to Chicago. She took days sorting and separating everything

figuring out what to take and what to give to family, friends, and

neighbors. Strangers walking along the road near our land sorted

through the stuff she put there for anyone to have and continue its use.

And then the day came when we prepared to say good-bye. It was a

gathering of extended family, and those who were determined to stay on

the land. It was a gathering of friends and people from around the land.

We gathered at Adam Pops Lakestone's grave. He was buried beside his

favorite tree. He grew this black gum tree from a sprig he planted so

long ago. He so loved when the tree produced its beautiful multi-colored

leaves as a seasonal change. It was a huge tree standing over 50 feet, full

of strong branches, and verdant leaves. How appropriate we gathered

here when the tree was full of its amazing flowers of white, yellow, red,

and orange. Such an unusual tree, which is why Pops was so determined to have his tree, on his land. The leaves covered the ground like a soft quilt fashioned by hand. The tree provided shade around the grave site. It was the same shade that comforted Pops when he came here to be at peace with himself. Words of comfort and joy were spoken. The gathering provided solace for everyone gathered. In the background, a Choctaw man beat a drum with an infectious rhythm that went straight inside of each heart. There was soft crying, even some laughter. The experience emotionally affected us all.

Very few words were spoken when we left to board the train leaving for parts unknown, unseen, transporting us to Chicago. Many people gathered at the train station. Just as many travelers were in the ticket area with the sign designating for White Only. We entered passing under the sign that read Colored. It was basically quiet with smothering tension where we waited. You could hear the muffled conversations. Children chattering as they played. Babies crying wanting to be held the right way. Babies can sense tension from the person holding them. The tension was manifested as fear. Fear of the unknown, the unfamiliar, the common ordinary that was not to be this day.

My father was obviously nervous thinking about reports of people being turned away after being accused of having forged tickets. This was another tactic of Jim Crow behavior just to disrupt the migration to

Chicago. Fortunately, all the tickets were stamped and validated. Everybody would board the train. After the ticketing drill the level of clamor increased in the waiting area. The tension diminished, and the adults talked freely and smiled openly with each other. The train arrived with a roar that frightened some. Suddenly, there was a rush to board the train. There was no problem finding the faded ugly green car with the bold lettering Colored Only.

Because we had all heard the stories about the train trip everybody had prepared food to share and enjoy along the way. Ma carried a sturdy box that resembled a fancy ribbon trimmed hat box. Inside was fried chicken, potato salad, deviled eggs, biscuits, and sweet potato pie. In another bag she had cloth napkins, little tin plates, tin cups and spoons, and a jug of sweet tea. She had also placed jars of fruit and vegetables she had canned from her garden. This was the common fare for all the travelers, and once the eating started so did the sharing. It smelled like a café once the food containers were opened. We all knew that it was uncertain where we would be able to purchase food on the trip up North. Our family had enough for a day and maybe half into the next day.

Directions from previous northward voyagers had spread the word about friendly colored folk who would sell food items at certain stations where there were white only eateries. It was worse finding toilet facilities during the trip. There were occasions when toilets weren't available on the colored cars. Most stations had designated toilets for stop overs when the train was being serviced, but our people had no place to relieve themselves. Again, without the aid of previous voyagers we would not have known about the friendly colored folk along the way, who provided comfortable means for our people.

The worse account about the whole trip was a tale about the devilish white man who rode the rail line looking to throw somebody off the train as it sped down the tracks. The truth of this story centered around a bad-tempered conductor who was known for threats to throw people off the train for not respecting his authority. It was said that he got angry and started bellowing at the top of his voice and looked feverishly red like pictures of the devil in children's story books. The stories mixed with fact and rumor said one day the conductor got so angry, that he pulled the emergency cord and stopped the train. The story goes that he swung open the door to the train, and physically forced a man off the train in the middle of nowhere. And then threw all the man's belongings off the train too. Attempts were made to dispel the stories, but the story about the devil conductor continued, as well as the understandable fear. So much so, that the tale seemed to expand on its own until it was embellished with throwing the man, his wife, and three children off the train. Some even added that he didn't throw their food off but stood in the aisle and ate it in front of the other passengers daring them to do something. No one knows what happened to the family after the train continued down the tracks. The belief and fear of the devil conductor continued to survive, long after on the rail journeys to Chicago.

My father found the stories about traveling up North entertaining and funny. He said they were like the newspapers since they were filled with bad news, lies, and innuendo. He said he was not afraid of no white man and wouldn't give the devil the opportunity to get him and his family kicked of the train. He was realistic about how he would handle any obstacles and would protect his family first at any cost. Come hell or the high water, he avowed. The stories my father talked about and laughed about the most were the ones about the cold and snow in Chicago, and especially the Chicago ocean. He would start off by saying "the story goes." He would have this sheepish grin as he told the story.

"The story goes," that this man from Mississippi moved to Chicago and froze right in motion as he was struggling to walk against the wind, down the snow covered street one winter day. He hadn't been in Chicago very long. Being from Mississippi he didn't have a proper winter coat, no hat, no boots, and no gloves. Suddenly as he turned the corner beside this tall building a strong gust of wind wrapped around him like it was his bear skin winter coat and froze him solid right there man!"

Then my father would shake all over as he laughed uncontrollably, tears rolling from the corners of his eyes. My mother would tell him to quit telling lies like that. Reminding him that the stories were exaggerations never stopped him from repeating the falsehoods. She would say it was sad to say somebody froze on the street, but in the end, she was laughing just as uproariously. Coming from Mississippi and adjusting to the winter weather in Chicago was a tremendous challenge experienced by many. The howling wind that bit the skin. The freezing cold that held your hands and feet like they suddenly were numb. And the snow so stunning, while controlling the movement of your life for days. It was a matter of learning how to deal with it all, especially most important, how to stay warm. Home in Mississippi got cold during the winter, but nothing like walking around in Chicago when the temperature stayed below zero for days.

An extreme shift occurred on a psychological and emotional level, once the train crossed the Mason-Dixon line. It was as if the grasp of Jim Crow thawed miraculously. It manifested in the story telling conversations on the train. Passengers were less tense and more relaxed.

Even though most people didn't believe the devil conductor story, there were true incidents when passengers were escorted off the train. But out of the perceived reach of Jim Crow, there was a cloak of satisfying safety. The excitement level was spontaneous, and anticipatory themes sprung forth amongst the passengers. I remember my father talking to another man when the conversation got very involved.

Seems like everybody wanted to talk about their dreams and aspirations being fulfilled in Chicago. One man traveling alone just started talking to my father. He was so sincere and committed to his beliefs about life in Chicago.

"Man, you know what? I will be so glad to be in Chicago. I can't wait to have my own apartment in one of those tall brick buildings. I want to live on the Southside, where all my friends and family live and walk down those wide cement streets. I will go to the Mount Olive AME Church the first Sunday I am in Chicago. I must go to that barber shop where all the news about Chicago was talked about and sent back to us down in Mississippi. And man! I can't wait to see that ocean in Chicago."

My father stopped him right then asking what he was talking about seeing the ocean in Chicago. The man became very animated as he described what he called the ocean. His eyes got wide, and he talked a little louder causing the other passengers near us to stop their own conversations and listen to the man.

"Yeah man! My cousin told me about the ocean that he went to in Chicago. He said there were huge waves that wash upon the shore where there is sand and lots of people having a good time on the beach. Yeah, yeah, they even call it the beach. I can't wait to be there and have a good time."

My father told him he had not been to Chicago before, but there is not an ocean in Chicago. He did not want to offend the man or make him look foolish. He suggested that maybe he was mistaking Lake Michigan for the ocean because the lake is gigantic. With kindness, he told the man that Michigan in Indian tribal language means big water. I wondered how he knew that. The tribes in Michigan are different from my grandfather's people. So how did he know about Lake Michigan.

 The man just looked at him with his mouth wide open, still wild eyed, slowly shaking his head from side to side. "But... it has a sandy beach man!"

****

Pastoral scene of the gallant south

The bulging eyes and the twisted mouth

Scent of magnolias, sweet and fresh

Then the sudden smell of burning flesh

"Strange Fruit" Billie Holliday

I'm sitting right next to Ma. I hardly noticed, but she has disconnected from me and the conversations. She looks forlorn and dejected. Asking her what is wrong or what she is thinking I suspect wouldn't bring forth her feelings. Only later did she reveal the tragic story that had frozen her in place like the Chicago winters. But, the event was in the sweltering heat of Jim Crow Mississippi. She had spent so much time swallowing the event, while gagging to keep it so deep down into her psyche, that recalling it that day, on the journey North was so unexpected and rude. Unexpected because denial had been her only ally, her benevolent protector from the hidden scars that penetrated her beingness. Like a lurking dark villain of malevolence, it quickly knocked down the high walls of denial, surrounding her in an invisible murky, nastiness she could taste. A bitter, oily bile. Rude, because it won in an unfair arena. She was unschooled, unprepared, naïve, and defenseless against its shadowy, sneaky appearance.

She was too young to grapple with gathering the right whispers to describe what she saw or to put a defining word on it. Later, she heard a word while people talked in fear and terror when they uttered lynch. When she heard the word, it was like a whisper of air from start to finish.

L Y N C H. She better understood the phrase... "dey hanged him."

That day was etched in her mind. The denial allowed her to squeeze it into a smaller and smaller shuttering corner somewhere else. But that took time. Before that time, she had so much terror, fear, sleepless nights that manifested the same screeching sound and images over and over. Sleep and hunger was stolen from her, even her ability to comfort herself. She became hypervigilant and apprehensive about everything and everybody.

"What was that!? Who's that in the hallway?

She lived in Tupelo Mississippi then. A small farming agricultural town inhabited most by colored folk. But the white man still controlled everything with Jim Crow rule and the rule that accompanied their white governance.

Cotton created textile mills and jobs for white only. The mills were in town. The colored folk were primarily rural. They maintain family and community within themselves and a few of the indigenous Choctaw and Chickasaw peoples that remained by crops sharing and cultivating.

Nothing can obliterate those images of such human humiliation and depraved destruction of a being and its complete essence. The numbness was complete and all-consuming from the core out to the surface, smothering the precious innocence of an impressionable 13 year old Elizabeth. Who or what could create this portrayal of cruelty at such levels of inhumanity. What vulgar victimization of this unblemished soul, accomplished with wanton pride.

According to Elizabeth she recalled the day when she and her auntie were walking home from a trip to town. They were so happy talking about the pretty accessories they had bought at the Five & Dime store. The two of them were making plans to refashion a couple of dresses to attend a church social. They were laughing, poking fun at each other and completely joyous. It was a typical sweltering 90-degree Mississippi day. The sun was still high overhead but moving towards the post noon hours. Not even a touch of a breeze to cool the evidence of the sun's heat appearing as waves on the horizon. Walking felt like struggling through invisible wet sheets of sticky heat. To complain just added weight to the situation of being so hot.

One specific detail that always lingers with Elizabeth about that day was the cicadas singing their mating calls. These were seventeen-year locust, as they are known. They aren't really locust or grasshoppers. They were so particularly prevalent that season. The sound of the cicadas put a hypersensitive impression on Elizabeth and her memories. Recall of that day brings forth the sounds before the dark images.

The two of them were just reaching the bend in the road where a huge black gum tree grew, known as the Tupelo Gum. They heard the cicadas as they approached, and the screeching singing of the locust got louder and louder. Blocking out all other sounds. The tree must have been overly inhabited by the locust shedding their exoskeletons becoming a bizarre alien creature

They had walked this same road, at this same spot, countless times before. Nothin but nothing prepared Elizabeth for the sight as they round the bend in the road overshadowed by the towering lush gum tree. Maybe the language of the cicada was crying out a warning to them. This very **distinct annoying sound that some say sounded like the insects were calling the Pharaohs.**

Pharaoh… phaaaaaraoooh… phaaaaaraoooh… pharaoh!

Auntie stopped abruptly and put one arm out in front of Elizabeth. She just softly said stop. Elizabeth's inborne curiosity drove her to look around, and quickly survey with sweeping glances in front and beside her.

"What? What's the matter Auntie?"

The aberration slapped her like a sudden lightning strike right between her eyes. Her lower jaw dropped, her eyes widened, her body became ridged and utterances were stalled at the back of her tongue. The entirety of her function was arrested as her mind and impulses began to compute and interpret what her eyes struggled to comprehend. In that instantaneous moment, the pharaohs sounded the alarm for her to escape, fly away, or!

Before them a shape with characteristics of a once human body hung from a thick rope noose knotted to a tree branch. The corpse was a charred onyx black configuration of a once breathing person. The lower limbs stopped with brittle burnt bone where the feet were supposed to be. The lower torso featured a gaping burnt hole, evidence of a malicious castration. The rest of the torso looked like flaking fried skin, and in some places burnt oozing yellow fat from the bulkiest bodily areas. Each fully burnt hand appeared taut and positioned like claws. The head was slackened devoid of distinguishable facial features. The burnt lips emphasized missing and broken grayish teeth. A thick coagulated juice oozed from the eye sockets, and a hole where a nose had existed. It was the utmost horrifying example of a human's inhumanity to the sanctity of creation for a young innocent girl to witness.

PHARAOL PHARAOL PHARAOL

Elizabeth dropped every one of her precious items she had purchased and started running. Still not uttering words or releasing fear filled screams. She alternated between running and walking very fast. She just needed to get home as quickly as possible. She tripped on a stone falling, but this didn't slow her down. She commenced crawling the second her knees hit the ground. Ripping her dress at the waist from crawling, she regained her balance, stood, and vomited violently, running just as fast again.

Auntie kept calling and calling after her niece while gathering up their shopping goods and attempting to catch up with her niece. But she couldn't, as Elizabeth was too driven to feel the security of home. To hopefully erase the aberration, to rub out the entire day. But that wasn't to be. Even the cicadas seemingly followed her, their intensity unrelenting and just as irritating.

Thousands of men, women, and children, over the years were lynched in Mississippi. Scores of others uncounted were never recovered by their loved ones. The scourge of the tragic murdering was so incomprehensible to foster the needed resolution, justice, and closure for thousands of families.

Elizabeth had heard of lynching, but it was her first time seeing and experiencing the full impact of it on her mind, body, and most of all her soul.

Auntie nearly caught up with her when she tripped again and landed on her face in the red Mississippi clay. As she attempted to stand, the trauma caused her to completely lose control of her bladder and soiled the tattered and torn dress that was already dirty from running and falling. Her dress hung in shreds from her waist.

She lost much more, including her will to continue, to survive. She was traumatized by the terror of the lynched man that she had difficulty just existing. Others had to groom her including bathing her, when she would let them. She picked at food placed before her, avoided sleeping, other than nodding and brief naps. She feared the nightmares dominated by images she couldn't wipe away. The bedroom became her shrunken world. She only left the room to go to the toilet. She feared looking out the windows and always requested that the curtains be drawn closed. Conversation with her was short and disjointed, while ending abruptly as she fell into a far-away mysterious stare. A wild look captured her face with dark circles under eyes, drooping from lack of sleep. Her hair stuck out from her head like a wild entanglement. It was matted to her head on the side she positioned her head while lying in the bed most often. "God please let me wake-up from this scary dream."

Her family and those who knew her wanted the sweet, compassionate, always willing to help little girl that they loved and missed. They felt robbed and cheated seeing her in the everyday condition that devoured her soul. They wanted her back just as suddenly when she psychologically vanished. The frequent question was is she back? Is she back? Family knew and held inscrutable belief that she was being held behind a hazy wall of terror and fear, that would collapse eventually. It wasn't in her to surrender and not fight back. Something had to awaken that familiar formidable, yet gentle will she possessed within.

Many church people came and prayed and prayed. Some just stood and stared, shocked that they weren't seeing the Elizabeth they knew and loved. They tried laying hands on her, but she fought them off. Her paranoid told her they were out to harm her.

The household knew about her sleeping habits, or lack thereof for any real, restful sleep. No one knew about the talking and walking during the brief periods when she did surrender to sleep. She was overwhelmed by certain occurrences in her bedroom late in the night. But in her weakened delusional state a defense didn't exist. Defense against what, or who?

There weren't too many nights that she escaped from her visitor. When she would say the visitor, she stopped and pondered the arrested corners in her mind where she had lost herself. At first, she hid under a heavy patch quilt Auntie had made for her. At night she only allowed her nose and mouth to be uncovered so she could breathe. She was adamant about not seeing anything, so her eyes remained under the quilt. Poor thing suffered from her own body heat and the profuse sweating under the heavy smelly quilt.

Her frazzled mind conceived a force she eventually accepted. She thought that it hadn't killed her yet, although it looked it planned to and soon. One night she decided to stop hiding under the quilt since nothing had happened. Of course, it was dark in the room, but the more she looked, and her eyes adjusted, she saw the aberration across the room from her. To study it completely and comprehend its intention was what she wanted and needed. Her delusional mind's scrutiny, with increased effort revealed that she was looking at the victim hanging in that tree. Her confused mind told her it was right there in the room with her.

"Oh Lord, oh Lord please protect me."

Several nights transpired bringing about Elizabeth's confidence to speak with the victim. She wanted to know why it was in the room with her. Did it have intentions to harm her, burn her body too? The more she talked to herself and asked questions the more secure she surprised herself with persistence. Her inquisitiveness triggered a little eagerness. She asked if there was something it wanted from her. Thinking that would be the reason it visited every night. During the day, she would think of questions to ask anticipating the next visit.

At thirteen Elizabeth didn't realize it, but this mental reasoning started to help her. Pulling her back. Allowing her to sense herself again even if in small increments. Pulling her out of the depression and lessening the fear. After using the toilet one day she noticed how unkept her hair was, and how awful she smelled. She felt sad that she had let herself go. This made her take in the rest of her appearance and she was so disappointed and embarrassed.

"How did I let myself get like this. Why didn't Auntie say something to me about it. I stink"

Since nothing happened drastically while with the visitor, she felt prepared. She determined that it was time to unravel this strange and annoying mystery occurring every night. She told herself that it was too much to keep going on this way. Knowing that it wasn't who she really was to be acting like that. Especially, talking to some dark strange aberration every night in the dark. Something was wrong with all of it, and she felt it deep inside.

No one in the house knew any of the awakening changes in her were occurring. Unfortunately, they had given very little hope that things would get better. That Elizabeth would come back and be well.

Auntie at some point would occasionally hear talking coming from the dark bedroom. She seldom entered the room unless she had an intended reason to be there. She was ashamed that she had given up trying to reach her niece. It seemed that asking questions was futile. It was easy to ignore it, thinking it was just another part of the psychologically loss of their cherished loved one.

It was the turning point that Elizabeth remembered most about that period in her life when it felt and looked as if everything about her was lost, gone to some unknown existence. The inspiration roared for her to come to attention. Her spirit had enough of the self-loathing and degradation. She was tired of being tired. She was tired of being stricken by fear. Most of all she wanted herself back. She would confront the visitor with what little power remaining in her fragile body. This miniscule spark of gumption felt encouraging to her.

The dark always holds the mystique of the unknown, unseen, and wills its power so fittingly upon its captured victims. But Elizabeth had decided not to be victimized any longer. She would muster her strength into her atrophied muscles to sit up in the bed. She didn't need the smelly, sweat soak patch quilt as a shield any longer.

"What do you want? Why are you here? I want you to leave now. You ain't the boss of me." Spoken as a defiant 13 year old driven to escape from her illusive capture.

Success at sitting up motivated her to slowly swing her legs over the edge of the bed. Glaring at the visitor she stopped suddenly imagining that it had moved, changed its position just as she had. This was an opportunity to gain more strength for the next advance. Planting her feet on the floor and turning on the light to rob the visitor of its tricky scheme.

The visitor always positioned itself in front of the antique dresser against the wall across from the foot of the bed. The dresser had an ornate mirror which, Elizabeth had not allowed her face to be reflected after becoming a prisoner of her mind.

She stood next to the bed while her weak legs trembled. She glanced up at the single light bulb hanging on its electrical cord from the center of the ceiling. How many steps would it take to reach the light switch? She took the steps. Elizabeth screamed as the light invaded the darkness of her prison. She fell to the floor on her knees weeping very loud and glaring up towards the dresser. What she saw was so astonishing. There wasn't a visitor of any form. The dark ominous aberration she so feared did not exist.

The loud screams alerted Auntie and she rushed into the bedroom. She found Elizabeth standing before the dresser, tears flowing from her eyes. But she was smiling. She inspected the neat pile of clean clothing Auntie had put on the dresser anticipating the day her niece would want to refresh herself. The smile came from her heart as she examined the dress Auntie had adorned with the accessories they had purchased so long ago. The dress hung from a small hook on the side of the mirror, giving the impression, in the dark, of a standing figure along with the folded clothing. It was all an illusion fashioned from Elizabeth's young traumatized mind when she saw the mutilated human hanging from a tree. The fear was fully internalized.

She slowly stroked the fancy dress with such tenderness, as her eyes found her own face in the mirror. Auntie put her arms around her as they looked at each other and wept in comfort and joy. Auntie held the dress up to Elizabeth. The dress became very significant for her. Nine months later she was baptized in it. This was the beginning of her spiritual recovery and transformation. She willed to God that she would be a devoted believer, as a faithful servant, and always prepared to say yes to those in need.

****

In a dangerous world, a realm of disasters,

a place of grief and pain,

A sensible man himself dangerous, more frightening than all

The social and political accidents that might befall him.

He was in a way, a specialist in survival.

Charles R. Johnson

Yes, for sure I am Marlon. Why would I stop to ask myself who am I? …

Marlon Lakestone, but what is drawing me to ask the question. Is this

craziness going on really me? What is happening to me? As I look

intensely at myself in the mirror I see many features that come from my

family. My earthy, ruddy, shade comes from Pops, my Choctaw

grandfather. I have a broad, sharp, prominent nose. That too from Pops.

I smile looking at my lips. They say I have my great, great, grandmother

Rebecca's big full lips. Her upper lip it is said had a light violet hue that

people mistook for rouge. Everything was natural about her. The way

she looked and the way she acted. I'm glad I got her lips. She is the

African motherland in me. How great it would be to know what part of

Africa my ancestors were stolen from. Kids in school use to tease me

93

about my lips, but now I appreciate them as a part of me. I wished that I could have talked to my grandmother Rebecca before she died. It would have been difficult to bring up her experience during slavery. Even though I wished that she could have spoken with me about it. I understand how intolerable it must have been just from Pop's reactions whenever her name was mentioned. She persevered for her children. Is my will to never give up from her?   I focus and just look deep into my eyes. Who is the man behind them? Who is the man there? I know these are Stone's eyes, my father. I quite calling him dad when I got older. I called him Stone like everyone else. Not out of disrespect, but love. I smile remembering how he got that name from the guys he used to jam with in the jazz band. It was when he became so animated playing the piano. "Adam is stone crazy man! That's why we call him Stone." My eyes, like his, are deeply set, and people say that they look straight into you. Just like they would say about Stone and Pops. Ma use to tell me when we lived in Holmes Mississippi, that Pops could see things in people. He seemed to have a sense about things, she would say, like he knew stuff. They are dark brown. So, dark that people ask me if they are black. I guess that is why there's a little uneasiness when they feel like I'm seeing inside them. I look at the bushy thick brows above my eyes, which help with the characterization others have. They called Stone handsome and

cool. Chuckling a little I see that same handsome cool guy in me too.

 Right now, I'm trying to see inside myself. Is there something I should

seek deep inside myself to recognize or speculate about? No! Hell, no.

Stop that shit Marlon. I know who I am. What about it?

When I smile, they say they see Ma in me. I like that. She is always so

sweet and calm. I need her. I need her to calm me down. Just being in

her presence is peaceful and protective. She always knows what I need

and helps me to see it too, no matter how much I resist. I always feel the

same approaching Ma's house. I should say our house meaning the

family house. But I haven't lived here in years. Stone really got his

dream in this house. He was intrigued by the Spanish influence in

California, especially in the style in which many houses were constructed.

He looked at so many pictures of houses with a Spanish motif

particularly in Los Angeles. We moved from the Southside of Chicago to

View Park in Los Angeles. Here it is. Nothing has changed. Ma keeps

it looking freshly painted with white stucco. You walk up and first enter

the walled courtyard filled with an array of potted plants. From the

courtyard, you reach the large wooden entry door with wrought iron

fixtures. On either side of the door are terra cotta planters with forever blooming red and white geraniums. When you enter the foyer, you walk across the dark hardwood floors that flow throughout the house except in the kitchen. It has a custom terra cotta tiled floor. All the doorways and window frames have arches. I love the fireplace in the living room with the hand painted tiles and the strong wooden mantle.

Man, so glad Mr. Jackson gave me the day off. I needed it. I need to talk to Ma. Zena wanted to come, but she had to work. No way I could talk with Zena and Ma together. They become talking machines. Quick, intense, and frequent subject changes. No putting it off any longer. Today I will talk to Ma. I know she is sitting on the sofa in the living room. Her reading glasses are on the end of her nose and I bet she is reading a spiritual transformational book of some kind. Curled up next to her is that big yellow cat that I loathed. I know for sure the feeling is mutual from that cat. The hate between us is palpable. He looks just like that yellow cat in TV commercials. What's his name? Oh, yeah Morris. Well, Ma's cat is named Peaches. I laugh because that name doesn't fit him at all. I think that's why he is such a tyrant. He doesn't like his name either. He knows he needs a name that fits how he acts, and how he perceives himself. He is just mean and a sneaky terror. Ma found him as she was leaving the hair solon. It was an unusual winter day in Los Angeles. A fast-moving low front swept across the city, unloading quick flashes of heavy down pours of rain, with strong gusting

winds. Ma saw this cold, wet, crying kitten huddled next to the building.

She picked it up and bundled it inside of her coat. At home, she dried

the kitten off, fed it, and nursed him into this cute little thing named

Peaches. Now Ma spoils him so much, and he takes that to mean he is

human and privileged. He has reign of the house. Look at him. He just

jumped up on the back of the sofa to look out the window at me. How

did he know I was coming for a visit today? See. I hate that cat. He is

so eerie. He knows how I feel about him which makes it worse and his

antics more obvious. I complain to Ma, but she just calls him and

cuddles him up, while he looks at me from her lap with those dagger

green eyes, while his tail swishes slowly. I have learned that the swishing

tail means don't even try it or get scratched. He must have just meowed

causing Ma to look out the window too.

"Hi Marlon baby. It's good to see you suga. Come on in. You are just in

time for some lunch. Where is Zena?"

I used the time for Ma to serve lunch, and our eating together, to buy me

time to arrange my plan to ask what I need to ask, and to say what I

really think is gaining a grasp over me. While we ate some of her

delicious homemade bean soup, garden salad, and slices of her famous zucchini bread, she was excited about getting ready for Christmas. She asked me for a day to go get her tree and pointed out that she had already pulled out five boxes of decorations from the garage. She said she especially wanted me to reach the nativity figures from a shelf too high for her to reach for her yard display. Every room in the houses will be decorated for Christmas very soon.

She left the table to get the iced tea she had forgotten. I took this time to decide that I wasn't ready and would bring up something as a smoke screen until I could reveal my anxiety and fear. As she sat the pitcher of iced tea down she made a statement before I did.

"Baby when was the last time you stopped to meditate? Don't answer. I think we should do that before you leave today."

I jumped right in after that and told her I knew what it was like for me to live in Chicago, but that we had never actually talked about it much from her experiences. Okay. Good stall I thought. Ma could go on forever with this. I'll interrupt at the right moment for her and for me.

"What was it like for me suga......... That was so long ago and so much happened. Some good and some bad. You know. Life was going on in all ways that it could."

I was surprised at what Ma had to say about leaving Mississippi and living in Chicago. For her it was very disruptive and tore her a part inside. She was at peace with the country life and Pop's land. She loved it just as much as he did and learned from him how to honor it. Rising in the morning with the sun in Holmes Mississippi was the pinnacle of her inner peace. She gave honor and thanksgiving to God and the earth every day. Her day ended with the same abundant praise for God and her life. She went along with her husband's desire for a new life, and great promise in Chicago. Survival of the family was more important for her than resisting the move.

"You know what Marlon? I hated moving to Chicago, and I hated Chicago itself. All of it."

This showed me Ma's true grace. She never cried, shouted, or protested. She carried on even though Chicago was so foreign and unrewarding for her. I was unaware that we had moved around so much once we got there. Always with a relative, or a friend of a relative, back to someone we hardly knew. For her it was always crowded, cold, and devoid of anything that stirred her peaceful essence. I remember now. Ma was always cold. In Chicago she still wore a sweater even during hot summer days. Just walking around was unpleasant for her. Laughing at herself she describes how she walked.

"I know I looked country walking like my feet were stuck on fly paper. People would stop and stare at me. I wasn't used to walking on something so hard. Adam would smile and lock his arm in mine and pull me along until I matched his pace. Come on Lizzie he would say. People are looking at us.

 She said she just couldn't adjust to all those concrete sidewalks with walls of tall brick apartment buildings filled with all kinds of noise spilling into the streets. Everybody knew everybody's business. Every day she longed for the quiet, peaceful country roads, the mix of sweet aromas surrounding her, and the sound of nothingness. Instead she smelled grease, all kinds of food cooking and burning, and the air never smelled fresh.

 Living so close together sometimes with strangers was so difficult for Ma. But I was very surprised to hear about how I didn't sleep well at night. I guess Ma spent a lot of time soothing me to sleep, giving me warm milk. I was amazed to know I had frequent nightmares and to hear I got up and walked in my sleep. I asked about the dreaming and found out that I didn't remember anything. Apparently, the dreams scared me.

Ma said the strangest thing was when I would sleep walk and she would wake up and find me standing at the foot of their bed on my father's side. I learned I was just standing there, eyes closed, not moving. I was guided quietly back to bed and fell immediately to sleep. This must have been another difficult thing for Ma to deal with in our unfamiliar surroundings. She didn't understand what was going on with me. She was confident that I would grow out of it.

Cooking brings her joy. She loves to cook, but sharing a kitchen back then was nearly an impossibility. Back home she didn't let anyone messing around in her kitchen, moving stuff, and using things the wrong way she would say. To take turns cooking in a small disorganized kitchen in a Chicago apartment was overwhelmingly debilitating for her.

"You probably swallowed some of my tears of sorrow. I cried while I cooked all the time. I'm sure my tears must have rolled off my cheeks into what I was preparing for us to eat." "Aww Ma! That's so sad. I didn't know about any of this…... Why didn't you" "I know, I know baby. I wanted everything to be all right for you. And I did my best to have that happen."

I guess it did happen in her mind when we finally got our own place to live. Stone found a small two-bedroom apartment on the second floor of a building that had four family units up and four down. The important thing was that it was ours. Still too small, but ours. Ma got her joy back in that kitchen where two people would bump into each other, but where she decorated and organized it with her own loving touch. I remember looking out the window above the sink when I washed dishes. I could see the back yard behind the building. There was a high wooden fence around the yard, where there was an old rusted out broken down car, with a big mean dog chained up to it. Ma wanted to plant a garden back there, but not with that dog Stone warned her. Exploring around in the hallway Ma found a stairway leading to the roof of the apartment building. She cleaned things up on the roof and eventually started a vegetable garden in a bunch of good sized pots. Her habit of peaceful humming came back as she tend to her potted plants and cooked some scrumptious meals.

"I got my place for my family." She said we were forced upon each other with all the black people on the southside and all the white everywhere else. Jim Crow didn't exist in the same way. Still segregation, discrimination, and prejudice, but they smiled when they did it she explained.

"Down in Mississippi the hatred was right in your face. The migration to the supposed promise land didn't fully exist in Chicago like most of us believed it would. I do have to say there were good things. Like better schools, and more jobs available with better wages."

She talked about Stone taking advantage of the work opportunities. He connected to the migration information chain. Word of mouth news and information was passed from relative to relative, from friends to friend, and strangers weren't left out. After a few hit and misses, Stone was finally hired on at Armours, the nation's largest meat packing house.

Stone had a link within the packinghouse. A distant relative worked there who had skills with butcher knives he acquired from Pops way back when. After Pops slaughtered a hog or cow he quickly butchered the meat appropriately for immediate use and preserving. The relative that Pops training was a stand out in the packinghouse. He was the only black man doing the job he held as a butcher, and many white men despised him for it.

"Hey boy. Don't be thinkin nothin. You got that good meat cuttin job, but I will always be better than you. Cause I'm a white man."

Stone started in the slaughterhouse, where the animals were killed, skinned, and hung on overhead hooks. He wore a long black thick rubber apron that fell below his knees. He also wore black rubber gloves and high rubber boots. All of this to protected him from the blood, bones, entrails, and feces, he had to push away with a wide flat shovel, to keep the floor free to walk across. It was difficult for him to get use to the smells, and the stench of what went with the slaughtering of hogs, cows, and sheep. He gagged and tried not to vomit for the first two weeks of work. He never ate his bagged lunch. He had a hard time drinking water because it seemed like he was swallowing the reeking smells that completely engulfed the whole area.

When he got home he looked and smelled so nasty. Ma said it was hard to be around him. Even after a bath the smell seemed to linger on him somehow. It was a job. It paid good wages and it helped him put together enough money to get our first apartment.

"You know? That man of mine worked hard. He was never late for work, never took off because he was sick, but he truly hated that job and that packinghouse. He did it to keep us going, and he knew that something bigger, and better would come. I burnt incense in the house all the time to fight that odor. I didn't complain too much because I didn't want my husband to feel bad. He was taking care of us with that job."

Ma's tone changed when she started telling me about Stone hanging out and playing the piano in night clubs and juke joints in Chicago. These places still brought disfavor for her just like back in Holmes where Stone got his start playing the piano. It brought him such joy and took him away from the bloody misery of his everyday routine at the packinghouse.

"I know all that night life didn't sit well with you when Stone spent too much time in the joints. But just tell me a little about how he even got started." "That was back then. Nothing I could do about it. I had to trust him. I prayed all the time for the light of divine spirit to surround him."

Strange that Stone really got his start in the Chicago jazz scene through the Pentecostal church. Ma explained that she found a church right in the neighborhood, and she was pleased that it was a Pentecostal since that was our church in Holmes Mississippi. Stone didn't waste any time offering his services to play the organ and piano with the church choir. The drummer that kept the rhythm for the choir befriended Stone right away. He recognized Stone's talent and together they took the choir to a higher level of skill and performance. Word got out about the choir and the Sunday service congregations grew to capacity. The pastor had to step up his performance as well to deliver a more dynamic message. The drummer eventually asked Stone if he knew about Bronzeville and invited him to go on a Saturday after choir rehearsal. Bronzeville was the location of black culture on the Chicago Southside. At first the area was called the Black Ghetto. The title of Bronzeville became the name because it was not insulting. Bronzeville had an affluent black middle class that lived and thrived on the Southside. It was the mecca of black musicians, professional athletes, artist, and literary celebrities. Musicians especially, became famous as performers on the Southside of Chicago.

In Bronzeville there was a phenomenon called the Stroll. The Stroll was just that. Where the South Siders strolled down the street to be right in the rendezvous of the bright light district. Jazz was prominent and notables such as Louis Armstrong and La Vern Baker headlined the popular nightspots. The action went on night and day and Stone fell in love with it like it was an addiction. He and the drummer walked the crowded sidewalks going in and out of the night clubs like they were on a mission. Stone was overwhelmed with the desire to connect with a piano in one of the night clubs. Stone was so envious of the performers in the clubs. He couldn't sit still, and was always tapping his finger on tables, or his legs as he sat and listen to the musicians. His favorite spot was the Club De Lisa. This night club repelled Jim Crow. It was integrated from the patrons to the performers who appeared always with enthusiasm. There was a code used to refer to clubs like the De Lisa. It was brown and tan, which indicated that it was integrated. Out of all the clubs, Stone wanted to perform at the De Lisa. The club stayed open 24 hours per day. Stone took advantage of this and didn't let being at the club interfere with home life or his job. He became familiar with the manager and even met one of the four Italian brothers that owned the club. He was at the De Lisa every weekend and got to know the inner workings of the establishment including the gambling that took place in the basement. Gambling wasn't something Stone wanted to participate in. One visit to the gambling clique was enough for him. He was too driven to earn money for his family, and determined more so, to keep it in his pocket.

On one ordinary weekend Stone was, as they say in the right place at the right time. His drummer friend needed to set up his drums for the night's gig. He asked Stone to assist him moving a couple of the drums from church to the De Lisa Club. While the drums were being set up Stone was compelled like a force to the big black lacquered grand piano on the stage. He plunked at a few keys and like it was his piano he sat on the bench and began playing. At first, he wasn't playing anything specific. Just a few familiar notes here and there. But then he started to slowly play Amazing Grace. Maybe mid-way through he began to improvise. He was pumping the pedals vigorously, sliding up and down the keys and playing truly in an amazing style. People started coming into the room to see who was mastering the piano and the keys of the rendition so remarkably. Stone didn't notice because his eyes were closed, his head bend back like it might disconnect from the rest of him, and his body was fully animated. He looked like he was in his trance like state. One of the De Lisa brothers walked in and approached the piano where Stone was still into the rendition of Amazing Grace.

"Hey who are you. What is your name and where did you learn how to play like that? "Pardon me Mr. De Lisa. I should have asked someone...... "That's no problem. Who are you and how did you learn to play like that?" "My name is Adam Lakestone Jr. and they call me Stone. I've never had a music lesson in my life. No offense but it just comes natural to me. Like breathing I guess."

"Well I think you are a genius and when can you start playing here at the De Lisa Club?"

From then on Stone was a regular feature in the De Lisa and rapidly gained a faithful following of fans. The De Lisa brothers showcased him every week and on special occasions when renown performers were on the marquee.

Suddenly, life took a turn for Stone in Chicago. A slew of unfortunate happenstances ushered in many adjustments for him. Painfully, the De Lisa shut down. It went up in roaring flames from a disastrous fire. The site became the happening thing on the stroll for many weeks. Some people just stood across the street from it and wept openly. Some alone. Others huddled in groups. They had lost a beloved family member. The stroll was in mourning.

At the Amours packinghouse, some unexpected mechanization changes eliminated positions including Stones. Stone didn't let all of this stop his life. He had an inner strength that wouldn't let him slide into dejection and depression. He found ways to sooth himself while playing the piano with all his passion and interpretational improvisations. He especially released and revitalized himself leading the choir to all levels of exaltation during two services every Sunday. He told everybody he was just waiting for his next blessing.

Ma and I were unmoving in a state of quietness. Ma had stopped talking and reminiscing about Chicago. She sat across from me peering into a world of memories. She looked troubled but also had a placid presence about her. I just felt incapable and could only keep my eyes on her for that perplexing moment. I didn't want to intrude on whatever it was she was experiencing. This went on between us for a good fragment of time.

"Ma it must have been difficult for us when Stone was let go from the packinghouse…. We don't have to keep talking about back then if it bothers you." "Oh…what did you say baby?" "I was just…" "I heard you Marlon. Yes, it was a bad time. I hated Chicago. Nothing about it gave me comfort. I wanted to be back on the land. Pop's land that brought me so much peace and contentment. All of that washed away on that long death train ride North from Mississippi. Oh, Marlon it was awful for me. Something died in me on that miserable train. And I tried to protect you as much as I could from the drastic changes we experienced moving, leaving our real home."

Things always seemed to have come easy for Stone. At some point after losing his packinghouse job he was hired as a waiter on the passenger train of the Burlington & Quincey Railroad. He hadn't ever worked as a waiter before, but because he was so gregarious, he knew somebody, who knew somebody with the right contacts that opened the way for him to get the job. He fit in well with the waiter work and had to learn how to maneuver serving people on a rapidly moving train as it rocked back and forth down the tracks. He was equipped to deal with rude treatment from white passenger who viewed him as a slave waiter and not a paid for hire waiter. His confident smile and smooth way of dealing with white people helped him avoid conflict. Not a submissive smile. Behind that knowing smile, he discerned more about their ways than they did about his. It's how he learned to survive discrimination and racism by knowing his adversary's intentions before they did. The adversaries were unaware of this maneuvering advantage Stone mastered so well. He dismantled attempts to degrade him before the perpetrator was aware of what had happened. But Stone was fully aware that many black men were murdered just for smiling at what somebody thought was the wrong way.

He was so excited when he was assigned to work on the Zephyr streamliner. It was an eye catching futuristic looking silver luxury passenger train that was part of the Chicago hub of rail service. When the train rolled in the stations it attracted so much attention with the gleaming silver engine and coaches. The Zephyr provided service from Chicago to Oakland California.

Ma was smiling when she said that's when Stone fell in love with California. He learned the ropes as a waiter and eventually switched over to the City of Los Angeles, another luxury streamliner passenger train that operated from Chicago to Los Angeles. The Union Pacific Railroad Company operated the City of Los Angeles trains.

"The first time Stone had a run to Los Angeles, there was no turning back. He was in love with Los Angeles. When he returned home he nearly broke down the door entering so excited to tell us that we were going to move to Los Angeles. He said he knew he could do well there and suggested that we start packing up right then." "Wow. Just like that huh."

"Marlon… I know you didn't come here to talk about Chicago and all of that back then. Did you? Come over here, sit next to me, and let me hold your hand. Go ahead talk about what it is you need to say." "That's my mother. You know me… Yes Ma. I'm really concerned and… I guess I'm a little nervous about it too. But first I just need for you to tell me about when Stone got sick."

"I don't understand baby. We talked about it when it was happening. I thought that you understood when we talked. You were okay and all. At least I thought that you were."

Stone never went to the doctor. He literally had to be unable to get out of bed, before he would take medicine and then he would take one of Pop's remedies first. Things started happening physically to Stone that caused him not to be himself. The most striking was when he avoided being intimate sexually. How debilitated this was for a man so full of virility that he had difficulty getting an erection. It was so hurtful for him than it was for Ma. She of course was very supportive, understanding, and prayerful of course.

By the time, Stone finally went to a doctor in Chicago to address multiple problems with his health he was diagnosed with prostate cancer. The hardest part about it was that it had been there for some time, undetected and the future of it was uncertain.

"Ma. I remember that you were always playing that record by Ella Fitzgerald. What was the name? The song has ended." "No. It was The Song Is Ended by Irvin Berlin. It was written for Ella Fitzgerald to sing. I loved the way Ella sang it."

"You were always humming it too, when you were doing things around the house are just sitting looking out the window. That song meant something to you didn't it." "I listened to a lot of Ella's albums. But, yes that song was in my heart. It brought sadness and joy at the same time when I listened to it.

Stone was so committed to his belief in receiving the blessing, being the blessing. that he could not comprehend that he was in an abysmal dwelling of denial. He freely espoused that God would deliver him and remove the foreign invasion of his body. He would secret himself away and speak Pop's old native language and could even be heard chanting quietly.

"I am… I am… I am"

Underneath the damaging denial was a growing mound of depression. During the day at work he was still the jovial good natured make everyone smile man. Being at home seemed to remind him of looming doom because he perceived himself as letting his family down. He blamed himself unfortunately, for being sick.

The diagnosis came before the move to Los Angeles. It was another difficult time. Stone was so unpredictable with different shades of depression. At times, warm and engaging, other times withdrawn and irritable. There were days when he looked disheveled and unkempt, which was uncharacteristic of him. He disliked what he was going through and felt remorseful about what it was doing to his family. He dreaded the high and low feelings that came upon him unexpectedly. The most difficult for Ma was when he withdrew into himself and wouldn't talk, hardly ate, no matter what she prepared for him. But he never missed a day of work.

Nobody wanted to accept that Stone would do anything to himself. Everybody wanted it to be an accident and that's how most spoke of it. But the police viewed it as a suicide attempt. First of all, Stone didn't much like Lake Michigan. He only went in the summer time for an outing because Ma insisted. He thought that the water was too cold and dirty. He hated the waves reminding him that there weren't waves in the stream where he swam back in Holmes. He felt cold from the gusty breezes coming across the lake even during summer months. He was always shivering but wouldn't put on a jacket under heavy encouragement from Ma.

So why? The police asked. The police were on their usual patrol of the beach. This night was so black and dark. Dark heavy low hanging clouds hid the moon, on this dismal night. They used their spot lights along the routine patrol of the lake shore. The driver stopped suddenly when his partner asked if he saw that. After a back and forth swipe, the spot light focused on a neat stack of clothing unattended on the beach. Further searching while out of the patrol truck revealed someone struggling in the waves of the rumbling lake that night.

Stone was rescued from the lake. He was completely naked, suffering from hypothermia, and nearly unconscientious. The police in their report after days of investigation ruled it a suicide attempt. With the tremendous support of Ma, and his friends, Stone recovered. Being hired on the railroad was the medicine he needed to give him a grip on the depression and give him a fresh start in life. Frequent travel across the country and experiencing something new every day was very exciting for Stone. The decision to move to Los Angeles made him happier than he had been in months.

"Ma. I think for you, that song is the story about you and Stone. Your love, your loss, and how you cherished everything about it. You still remember. That song takes you back especially to the good things that happened. Sometimes while you were listening and humming along with it I wanted to know what you were seeing and feeling. Am I right about that?"

"Yes, Marlon you got it right. That song meant a lot to me and it still does. I liked it because it was both joyous and melancholy at the same time. Someone else may have heard something entirely different. Yes, it reminded me of my husband Adam, and I still to this day miss him. I guess that's why I would listen to that song. To bring him near, you know baby? I have a bunch of old LP albums packed away somewhere in the garage. I wonder if I can find it. Maybe you can help me look one day. We can listen to it together. Marlon let's not wait any longer and walk around our words. What's not right with you baby? Come on talk to me. You have been stalling much too long baby. When have you ever had reason to be afraid to talk to me?"

"I don't know Ma. Something hasn't ended for me. Remember when Stone was dying, and I was having those dreams and terrible nightmares. I thought I was going crazy. It was disturbing for Zena too. She had to deal with it right along with me. I put her through too much and I can't do that to her again. But it feels like it is here again. I had one of those nightmares just yesterday. They are not happening at night, they happen any time for some reason it seems. And I'm so afraid. Why is this happening to me again? I can't take it Ma."

"Okay Marlon. I hear you... Afraid of what baby? Fear of what? What it means? What could happen? You think you are going crazy? Just slow down. Don't let this fear control you like before. So just what is fear Marlon... Huh?... Think about it. Fear is just false expectations appearing real... f e a r... Okay, I know that is easier said that's done, but."

"But Ma. That doesn't stop the dreams from happening. That doesn't stop me from thinking who I'm dreaming about that could die like Stone. Even though I realize that is crazy thinking. You? Zena? Is it about me? I know Zena will freak out if she knew how much this is occurring again. She will insist that I drop some pills and see a therapist tomorrow. I don't want to upset her, but I won't do pills for sure. That haze from the meds won't work. Not now. I went through a lot when Stone died. I don't know if there is enough in me to survive that again. I can't do it Ma. I just can't be that again."

Ma started praying. I didn't hear her words because I wasn't listening. I was flung back to the time when the dreams started plaguing me. Eyes closed, I was not tuned in to Ma's prayer. I was seeing and hearing the strangeness of a miserable time in my life years gone by. I remembered a period when Stone was just not himself. He was sick more, and more often. Not like sick in bed but, just sick like his energy was drained. He definitely was not the happy go lucky enthusiastic Stone everyone knew and loved. Although he tried hard to present a front, he couldn't pull it off and it was noticeable. He was not himself, just so grumpier than anything. He seemed weaker too, complained of being stiff and frequent backache pain.

That's what he called it. He would just say IT when he talked about being sick. He wouldn't say the word cancer, as though if he did he was relinquishing power to the disease. He was given the cancer diagnosis before the move to Los Angeles. The doctors gave him information and advice, but he decided to do nothing. This wasn't too far off from advice that he could wait and see what developed before considering a treatment course.

So, time passed and who knows what was going on with the cancer. Stone always tried to be himself. When he couldn't go to work, worry set in. My worry. I took on the worry. I internalized the worry as my trepidation. I accommodated him by not saying he shouldn't do things and especially telling him he couldn't do something. Nobody told Stone he could not do something.

But when he started stumbling that was the turning point. He would force himself to go to work. Even though I knew it wasn't the best thing for him. That was his joy working in the dining car on the trains. He started needing assistance to climb the high stairs to board the trains. Finally, he had a major fall on the train. He dropped a tray of food in the dining car, which splashed all over several passengers who were eating. It caused a big uproar. He was told not to come back to work until he had a release from a company doctor.

He put up a fuss saying it wasn't his fault that there was something spilled on the floor by another waiter. He protested that he had many years when he didn't miss a single day of work. Which was true. I could see that he wasn't accepting what was taking place with him. He was, and he wasn't. He was in denial and didn't want to accept that he was seriously ill.

He didn't sleep much, and I didn't either. I started staying up later and later using excuses that I offered to Zena. I used my key board as a diversion and improvised many unique piano scores. It helped to mask the stress and worry that was overcoming me. To deny the depression seeping in.

The marriage suffered. Zena was understanding because she was aware that the cancer situation with Stone was serious. She took an analytical point of view, which was comforting for her. She tried not to be, but she was a therapist first.

She wasn't as close with Stone as she was with Ma, but she loved him too. It hurt her to see him not as she knew him to be. She felt helpless with all that was going on, especially with me. She kept pushing for all of us to enter therapy. For me it was like losing hold of what was happening with everything. I felt powerless over everything!"

It was Zena who used her sweet approach to get Stone to agree to go see the doctor. We all decided to go to the doctor with him. This lifted his spirit but at the same time made him feel awkward and uncomfortable. Stone didn't like losing his manhood. This felt like he was being babied.

There were a few appointments with the doctor. After some testing and multiple lab results the doctor requested that we all return. We were in the doctor's office while he went over the test, the results, and presented some statistics which were meaningless for where we were emotionally.

He finally looked at Ma, and said he was sorry but the cancer had metastasized. I didn't know the meaning of the word at the time. But since, I haven't ever been able to speak that word without it getting stuck, leaving me mute.

I would have trouble falling asleep many nights. Some nights resulted with me ruminating about the word I couldn't speak which I think triggered the awful dreams. Dreams that repeated over and over and got more detailed as I continued to lose sleep. Zena told me that I was having a sleep disturbance and that being deprived of sleep wasn't a good thing for me or my health. She worried that if it continued my mental health could be in danger. Her mental health was impacted just as much.

Closing my eyes meant seeing shadows and eventually manifested dreams with someone following me. I was running and running down dark foggy streets and alley ways trying to get away from this menacing figure. It was always imposing in the dream. The figure was always right there behind me so close and frightening. I would awaken in a panic state gasping for my breath. Agonizingly, the terror would start up again right where it left off when I would doze off again. Not deep sleep, because I knew I was dreaming again. The same moment. The same menacing figure was pursuing me. Right there close enough to capture me.

Hardly a full night of sleep ever gave me the rest I desperately needed. The dreams moved into nightmares and tangible terrors of the night. I found myself nodding off while driving, frequently at mid-day during work hours, and just about any time I settled down.

The most difficult reoccurring dream really took me to the edge of control. Leaving me feeling completely helpless, asking myself if I had lost it. Surprisingly, there was a period when the nightmares stopped. Seems like at the time I was visiting Stone daily. The visits took place either early morning before going to work, or after work before going home. I would bring a thermos of coffee for us, even though he only took one sip of his cup. On weekends, I went over while Ma was at church. I stayed, however until Ma arrived at home. This allowed me to focus entirely on Stone. We didn't talk about the cancer, because the introductory word was still IT. Saying it didn't give the cancer credence. So why say the word to allow existence.

Stone and I sat in front of the fireplace while talking. He always felt a chill and always had a fire going no matter the weather outside.

Sometimes there were just glowing cinders. Most often he had several logs in flames. The house was always too hot for everyone else.

It was a comfortable conversation with Stone when he reminisced about Pops and the land back in Mississippi. He said Adam Lakestone Sr. was the greatest man he ever knew, and he wanted so much to be just like his father. He outlined all the things he learned about life from Pops. He felt sad that he didn't make the time to pass these things on to me. I didn't know what to say after he confessed this. I always considered him a good provider and a great father, regardless of his view.

My jaw dropped, and my eyes widened to let in all the light of understanding, when Stone spoke of a still born child. Ma had delivered the baby before I was born. He fell silent while he stared deep into the flames of the fire. No sound, except the crackles from the smoldering fire. Softly, he started again and indicated that he had wanted a house full of kids with at least five boys. Nothing about the significance of five, or why there weren't other children.

"You are the only child I got Marlon. My only son." This left me speechless and very sad for him. He reached his arm out to me. Hugging was not his thing, but he made this one make up for all those he reluctantly held back. I could feel how his muscular body has shrunken. This frightened me, and total sadness washed over me.

The regular conversations continued and so did the deterioration of Stone's health. He walked hunched over by now, and it was evident that he was always in pain. The invasion of his digestive system weakened him further exacerbated by his refusal to eat. He did have unpleasant symptoms after eating and always resulting in prolonged vomiting. He argued, which was better. To eat or not to eat.

By this time, I had finally agreed to Zena's persuasions to enter therapy. I had to agree that I wasn't doing well from the extended sleep deprivation and night terrors. I felt nervous and jittery all the time. Very edgy. I woke up every day with a heavy load of despair. Then lugged the despair behind me reluctantly throughout the day. Everything bothered me to the point of snapping suddenly. The worse was the paranoid ideation that created periodic suspicions. Trust and comfort with others was frozen inside.

I took the prescribed medication. Zena argued that I didn't give it enough time to work, since I felt the same but even stranger. I argued what was the use although I was secretly taking the meds irregularly. I positioned that the dreams had stopped since talking almost daily with

Stone. She didn't see the connection. I didn't admit it but didn't see it either.

The sicker Stone became the more obstinate and unpredictable he was. Understandable, since he was losing control. He would exert what little power he had. Rarely did he eat anything even though Ma always had his favorite food simmering on the stove. So unpredictable when he would demand a plate of food and protest when he felt he wasn't given enough. Predictable when he had to rush to the bathroom to relieve from vomiting, or diarrhea.

No one expected Stone to get dressed and leave the house alone. Especially, during one of those unusual rain storms in Los Angeles. One of those storms with the rain coming down sideways from powerful winds bending the palm trees over like twigs. And it was bone chilling cold, for Southern California.

Ma arrived home from grocery shopping to find the front door standing open. She dropped the groceries right in the foyer, rushing through the house shouting Stone's name while searching every room. The sound of a siren and the flashing red lights of the paramedics caused her to rush back to the front door. She rushed down the street to where the flashing

lights lead her. Stone was lifted onto a gurney and into the ambulance.
He was rushed to the hospital and admitted in guarded condition.

Stone was hooked up to IV's and a feeding tube. He received excellent
care. But he was still cantankerous and wouldn't cooperate with the
nursing staff. His doctor said that his body was to emaciate of strength
and energy to fight back. This coupled with his lack of will, gave a
disfavored prognosis. It was a bleak reality.

It was hard to look at Stone. His face was sunken, dull, and his eyes were
forlorn. He was no longer the stocky, muscle toned, strikingly handsome
man that once had a smile for everyone. Was he shrinking right there
lying mostly in the fetal position. His frame revealed an extremely
defeated body. Lack of good nutrition and a destroyed digestive system
resulted in weight loss. No one would speak aloud that Stone was
wasting away.

The daily visits continued. In a sharp snap and without warning, Stone
wanted to converse again. Each visit involved a far-reaching story about
something from the past. These stories were like a chronical from
Holmes Mississippi and Pop's land, to the terrible experiences on the Jim
Crow train to Chicago, and his most fulfilling events in Chicago playing
with the greatest artist of jazz and blues in the Bronzeville clubs.

I hated the truth when the dreaming started again. At first just typical stuff that was remembered sometimes and other times not. Dreams flowed of course that weren't remarkable. Just typical dreams. Waking up was still heightened with depression and looming doom. The presence and reality of Stone's condition never diminished.

Then one day, Stone started saying remember when we did so and so and remember when we... He started each story this way, as if he really wanted the story to be significant and remembered. It was so sweet to see him smiling when he said remember when. I wanted to rush to his bedside and hug him. To hold him without fear of one salted tear escaping. That would anger him.

It struck the heart knowing and seeing how he used to be. How he gave his smile as a gift. The reality was, he was trying to give this gift now, because he was coming to terms with his death. He was coming to terms with his fate and wanted to say goodbye with the knowledge that he was a good father. The father and husband who tried his very best to be a good provider. He especially wanted his only son to know how much he was loved, and their time together was the best gift that a father could ever receive.

Each time after the stories and visits, leaving the hospital was overwhelming, and difficult thinking if it was the last. There was no reality. Everything was in a dark rumbling cloud of confusion, fear, and uncertainty. Making it through another day was always gloomy and unpromising.

How could he say I don't want you to visit so much? It stung! It was an act of enragement to hear this from him. But that stubborn side of Stone was still there. Once he made up his mind about something there was no changing it. I had to suck it up inside with all the other burning miseries deposited there.

"Don't come so much son. I don't want you here when it happens. Please! It's what I want."

When it happens? He is saying he knows he is dying and is ready. Ignoring him never worked. He became firm in his convictions for what he wanted. Ma in her compassionate ways, backed him up with his wishes, I'm sure they had their talks about this. She did not want to, but she also had to resolve herself to his anguished wishes. It felt wrong. Who ever heard of not visiting someone in the hospital. Someone who was dying. I still went. I didn't let him see me, but I had to see him, even from a distance.

Guilt and sadness was the best description for these unfamiliar dealings. Preparedness does not exist for such requirements that don't fit with who you are and how you feel about a loved one.

There weren't any choices, no options, nothing to do but relent to Stone's wishes to not visit him. Days were over shadowed with depressive gloom. I was feeling loss of self and impending loss of a beloved father. Nights were worse. Staying up to avoid the demons of nocturnal slumber. Less and less sleep meant more agitation and all the other unpleasant symptoms that followed. Waking hours were dreadful. Hours meant for sleep were punishingly unrelenting.

Thinking it might help. A double dose of sleeping pills sought to capture a few hours of peaceful sleep. Instead sleep on that night ushered in a prison of horrible terror. The needed sleep amazingly came slow and comforting. As sleep flowed it carried with it a consciousness of being pressed down, constricted in place on the bed. A strong feeling of restraint. Rapid thoughts. Unable to move. Unable to move. Struggling to move. Wake up. Trying to wake up. Please wake up. Can't move. So dark and scary. A silenced constricted yell to stop. But inaudible. Stop! Help me! Unable to move. Being pressed down on the bed. Wake up! CAN'T MOVE! WAKE UP! Suddenly, a face appears in the surrounding smoky grayness in the dream. Surreal. So, shocking when a shadow of a face appears up close. Appearing so close, nose to nose. So, close. Hard to distinguish the features of the face. So, close can't move the fear away. Struggling and struggling, when the face vanishes into a solid blackness. Can't breathe. Can't breathe. Hyperventilating in the dream with the ever-present invisible weighted force of being pressed down on the bed. No. NO! The face reappears. Struggling ceased when the awareness and recognition revealed that the face appearing in the smothering darkness is Stone's face. Instantaneously, I am awake still hyperventilating gasping for a breath.

That morning, a determined decision was made to disregard Stone's demands for no visitation.

You told me not to come so much. Not to visit you because you didn't want me there when… I know now. And I'm on my way. Maybe I can make it there in time. If only I can.

Arrived at the hospital before actual visiting hours. Hospital staff too busy with change of shift reports to notice me entering. I walk with urgency not to see, but to release the knowingness inside my entire body. My body is tense and relaxed at the same time and I feel a feverish heat surrounding me. The hospital room of multiple shades of monochromatic white holds no secrets from me. I see Stone. Face so peaceful and content, his eyes partially opened. The once powerful arms now withered and folded across his chest... And I know.

"Excuse me nurse. Please come to my father's room. I think... he just died."

****

I open my eyes to see Ma still praying. One of her long prayers. My hand holding her hand is very moist from the lengthy contact. My hand is trembling slightly.

"Amen. And so, it is. Whew! That was a powerful prayer. I don't know where it came from. You all right baby?" "Yes, Mrs. Lakestone. You helped me. Just what I needed to confront this fear and a lot of other stuff going on with me lately. I needed to be here in this house today...Thanks Ma. Hey how about we go pick out your Christmas tree. One of those like Stone would like that touches the ceiling."

The day spent with Ma was fulfilling and enlightening. Actually, it was more than I anticipated. I needed to face up to everything, especially my fears. I have a little time left to finish dinner before Zena comes home.

This will be a relaxing Friday evening, starting with dinner and honest talk with Zena. I owe that to her.

I just had enough time to prepare pasta, a nice creamy shrimp sauce, some garlic bread, and open Zena's favorite bottle of wine. This should be a nice evening together. I want us to enjoy it and be relaxed with each other. I know she has missed our usual love making. I've been too tense and out of my head. Just about a lunatic. I'm glad I can say that to myself. More importantly, I will say it to Zena as best I can. I love her so much, and I know she loves me more than I deserved lately.

She is here. I'm not ready, but I guess I have to be as ready as I ever will be.

"Hi Mar. Uum. What smells so good? You cooked dinner? Wow!"
"Come here and give me a hug babe."

I hugged her so long it becomes obvious that something was going on with me. But I am just gathering myself. I have so much to tell her. Some tough shit to reveal.

"How was your talk with Ma today? How is she doing? Did it help Mar?"

I loosen my arms around Zena enough to look her in the face and those piercing yellow speckled eyes that are wide in anticipation. Her analyzing mind is already at work and I must head it off by overloading her with information. The truth. "Zena remember when Stone was dying and told me not to visit him?" "Of course, how could I not remember all of that Mar."

I tell her how I was so traumatized by Stone's illness, and the fact that I was powerless to effect anything to change the fact that he was dying. She knows this because she insisted that I see a therapist. No one knew back then how close I was to losing my sanity. Not even Zena sleeping right next to me as I swirled in a dark world of dreams and visions. I struggled to ignore the dreams. To control them, but most to understand what they were saying to me.

"Zena remember when I honored Stone's demand that I not visit him because he didn't want me to be there when he was dying? I did honor his demands. What was it inside of me that urged me on to rush to his bedside to find that he had just died just a few minutes before I arrived. What was that Zena? It was like a shock of electricity that shook me and right then I knew. I knew Stone was dying Zena. Later, I do know it made me feel connected like I had some instinct or something. But why me? I guest that's odd to say. Why not me!"

Zena looked mesmerized by what I was telling her. She was holding on to me tighter now with her arms around my waist as we stood there together. I told her that talking with Ma helped me to realize that I allowed fear to dictate my responses to everything that had been happening to me. I was overwhelmed with such fear that everything became distorted and confusing. I explained that it got to the point that I didn't know what was real, other than the fact that my father was dying from cancer.

"And Zena, that brings us to today. Come let's sit on the sofa." "Oh Mar. You are scaring me baby. What is it?"

Revealing this was not easy. I wanted not to be in this position. But for my sake and especially Zena's it is necessary. First, I let her know that her recent suspicions have been right on target. She is right. It is like before, but the last few days have been worse and so difficult to endure. I believe what Ma said to me about our abilities that we have forgotten. We humans stopped used the abilities, so when they appear the first thing we think is, this is crazy. We ignore the sense of what we know. All of us from time to time have said something told me not to do that. We have the ability to sense things. Ma described it as our spiritualistic rhythms. She spoke about how animals know when an earthquake is coming. Why wouldn't we have the same ability since we are more advanced than say a cat. But sometimes I really know that her cat Peaches is aware of me way before I enter the house. It's funny but true.

We as humans have become disconnected. We lost the rhythm, the connections inside of us to have the wisdom to sense the unseen. I was worried that I was becoming too deep with Zena and this stuff about sensing. I don't want to frighten her more than she already looks like she is. I must lay it all out in the open.

By now we are at the dining room table. Our plates are served with the pasta and we continue to talk. I talk mostly while Zena sips her wine nervously. I don't have an appetite for this delicious food I have prepared. I just want to move forward since we are into this.

"Zena. I don't want to scare you anymore that you are, but I have more to talk about... Do you think we have the ability to know and sense things in advance of something happening?"

I take my glass of wine and scoot my chair at the table right next to her. She says nothing, but her eyes just look with intensity. I tell her that in one of my recent dreams, my Choctaw grandfather appeared in a foggy mist. Pops didn't say or do anything. The dream continued, but Pops went out of focus. The strangest thing was when I heard a whispered word somewhere in that fog. That word was chicamungua. I've heard Pops speak a word or words similar. But what they mean, I didn't know, until I found a book on languages. It's something about water. Zena still looked at me with alarm. I continue.

I was in a state of dreaming but having the awareness that I was dreaming. Therefore, I was asking myself about that word. There was a strong feeling of knowing, but right there in the dream I couldn't recall. I tried so hard that I found myself struggling to wake up. I felt like an invisible powerful weight was pressing me down into the bed. The struggle found me gasping for my breath. I awoke covered in sweat and shivering.

"This is an important question I have for you please… What if I wouldn't have reacted with fear of the dream and the visions in it? What if I would have reacted like I knew exactly what was happening and connected with Pops? What if that word was a message because I wasn't connected? What am I supposed to know?" "I wished that I knew Marlon. I want to help but I don't know what to say or do." "That wasn't a question for you. I'm asking myself without the fear. The fear clouds the dreams and it either moves in slow motion and you never reach anywhere, or anything, or jerking and out of control like a movie that speeds up the frames. Of course, dreams don't mean what they look like. We know that much. But are they windows of awareness? I'm asking myself all of this."

I get serious now. Talking low and slow to Zena. It didn't take much for her to go back with me to those terrible days when I was powerless to depression, delusions, sleep deprivation, anxiety, and stifling fear. It is no secret. It was all about Stone's death, and how it impacted me.

"Zena… When this all started again I immediately though… who is going to die. Can you understand how I went to that train of thought?"

I reassure Zena that that is not where I am today. That I have the fear under control. At least recognizing the impact of it is the first step to mastering it. I point out that yes, I was also thinking, was Ma going to die, and yes even shared that I feared something was going to happen to her, my wife. Maybe a tragic accident or a sudden illness taking her away from me.

"Zena. I keep saying this. I don't want to scare you. Be with me on this. Let's see… Let's just call it intuit. Sensing. I'm saying I must follow the intuition I feel. There is something. I don't know what, but I can feel it.

Sense it. Something. What's wrong with thinking it is something good this time? I'm feeling there is something. Something for me to do."

"Okay Marlon. I have heard what you wanted to tell me. Right now, I can't take in any more. Can we let it rest for now? You know I'm not going anyplace. . . What's today? December…. thirteenth and the year is coming to an end before we know it. Okay tomorrow is the fourteenth of course, and the middle of the month with just two weeks before Christmas. Ma said she wanted to finish her shopping this Saturday. You know she likes to go to Fedco over there on La Cienega on Saturdays as busy as it is. But let's do it with her. I still have some gifts to buy too. It will be fun for us all. A nice break that we need. Huh?" "Okay babe. I love you and thank you. . . Yeah, let's do that with Ma. But please don't make me eat one of those big nasty grilled hot dogs everybody likes from Fedco." Even thought I had much, much more to share with her. I agreed to give her some relief. It was too much for her. I couldn't put Zena through any more... I was still hyped up on what I was experiencing, and mostly the insight that was overwhelming me with something I should do. Something I had to do. I couldn't turn it off, and the evening continued. I had to give her a break or break her. We snuggled on the sofa together while the television watched us. We certainly weren't interested in what was on the screen. Even the wine had lost the familiar taste and buzz we enjoyed. Finally, we headed off to the bedroom. Ordinarily, some good sex would have been in order. The tension still surrounded us.

As soon as Zena's head hit the pillow she started chattering about work. She was avoiding her lingering fear brought on by my revelations in the dreams. She had the perfect topic to direct the tension and anxiety. I didn't need to ask what was bothering her. Policy changes at work gave her space to release. She was so animated about the increase in paper work, more forms to complete, and still having to spend the same amount of direct service time with her clients. It was fine with me because I was distracted too. I would give an approving grunt, and a few umm hums here and there to imply I was listening to her.

"Zena. Can we talk about tomorrow to make sure we are on the same page? What time are we leaving? Who is riding with Ma? What last minute things do we need to remember to pick up? You know how Ma shops. We need a plan. It's going to be really crazy at Fedco on Saturday."

I said all of this as a deflection, and to buy me time. I can't let the feeling go that something is… I don't know how to even think to call whatever it is. Maybe if I just settle down and let it… Let it what? I wished that I could just figure out the what, and the it, of this shit going on. But being angry and upset won't give me clarity. Right now, would be the perfect time to meditate with Ma to get in touch with myself. But instead I continue to listen as Zena found solutions to all the questions I had just presented about Ma, and tomorrow. Instead I'm tossing and turning, trying to find my comfortable spot. I realize Zena must have found her comfort, because I hear her heavy breathing. She is deep in sleep.

The Third Day

December 14, 1963

The very time I thought I was lost, my dungeon shook
and my chains fell off.

Anonymous

How much time passed? There is no way for me to know but I am asleep as well. I'm dreaming, and I know it in this lucidity between reality and a trance like state. I want to wake up to gain control, but the dream is playing, and my eyes won't open. I'm talking to my father Stone. He looks so forlorn and out of character. He is sad. Not his usual jubilant, outgoing self. I feel sad having no choice but to look at him. He is wearing what he used to call his lookin' good, shark skin suit. That shiny silver suit he used to dress in, when he performed in the jazz clubs in Chicago. Suddenly, he jumps up and begins to run. I follow trying to keep up with him, but he is unusually fast. We are both thrashing through tall thick brush and over hanging branches that almost slam into my face. I can no longer see him, but I keep running although I am having trouble breathing and my legs won't move. Suddenly, we are both back where we started seated at the same table. Stone looks up at me and turns his head to the side and points. I look at him, and in the direction where he is pointing. I can't see anything in the brilliant nothingness where he points. He continues pointing and then starts speaking rapidly. I can't understand anything he is saying because his words are distorted. It sounds like the words have been slowed down and emanating from an echo chamber. He is upset because I'm not comprehending. He slowly fades away like a whiff of smoke. I'm left alone at the table.

"Wake up Mar. Come on wake up. I have breakfast started. Come on my sweet man. Time to get up."

I feel so strange. How long was I sleeping? Did that dream last all night? What did it mean? And that was Stone I was chasing… Oh my God!

"Okay, babe. Let me go to the bathroom first and I will be right there."

I look at myself in the mirror. I feel all right. Not like other times and other dreams. I don't feel that controlling fear. I'm not scared of some unknown. I know I can't read something into that dream other than maybe some carry over concern about… Yes, about what? I smile at myself in the mirror thinking about my father. That was all right seeing him. What a surprise visit. That was so funny now that I think about it. How was he able to run so fast? Where was he going so fast? And why?

"Marlon. I'm outside the door man… When did peeing become such a funny experience? I can hear you laughing. Come eat. NOW!" "You can't stop me from laughing, because I'm still doing it. You make me laugh all the time. But all right babe. Here I come just drying my hands." I laugh again telling her I love her bossy ass so much.

It's like 7:30 AM on a Saturday morning and I'm sitting across from my wife eating breakfast, wondering why I'm not still in bed. Oh, I get it. Zena and Ma are going to be together today. That's always a tour de force for activity, commotions, and of course the unanticipated. They have no set agenda other than let's go. I just get dragged along in the afterburn. Man! What's going to make it worse today is the frantic crowds fighting for Christmas bargains. With just weeks to go before what should be a day remembering the birth of Jesus.

This feeling that I should do something is nagging me. Really deep in my gut. So much so that I'm willing to face the wrath of my wife and mother to reconcile. Damn! That's why just going on an endless shopping fling won't work today.

"Babe I really need to deal with something this morning. I'm asking if you can accept me meeting you and Ma near lunchtime over at Fedco rather than standing in that crowd of people before the store doors open."

Shocking that she didn't put up a big fuss about my request for understanding. Her request was only that I not keep her and Ma waiting. She emphasized just please being on time. This was a gift not expected. She was so agreeable and understanding. Okay. That's the direction for me to go with the strangeness of this premonition stirring inside me. To be agreeable and understanding. No questioning. No doubting. Sitting here for the last hour trying to feel comfortable with not knowing what's next for me to do. But still there's the dream about Stone drawing me to question. Suddenly, I decide to pull out the family photo albums. That image of Stone in his favorite shark skin suit seems to be fascinating me. Turning the pages is like a rapid journey back seeing family members, events, and gatherings. It feels good crossing through cycles of family happiness and sadness. The sadness comes from recalling what was taking place in certain pictures. Like the pictures from the repast for family and friends at the church following Stone's burial.

Here it is. I found it. Stone's picture in the shiny silver shark skin suit. He looks sharp as a tack, as he would say. He also looks jovial, smiling, and posing with one hand in his pocket and one on his hip, head back and tilted to the side. He knows he is looking good. Smiling back at him feels good too. He is embracing me with that smile. I feel so, so… I can't come up with the word. Holding the picture up for a closer look, another photo that was stuck to the back of Stone's picture falls in my lap. It's a black and white photo of me and Ma sitting on the steps of the front porch of our house back in Holmes Mississippi. At the bottom is my name printed in pencil in little boy script. I guess I'm around 8 years old. She has her arm around me as I grin with a wide admiring smile looking up into her eyes. She considers my face with such love and compassion. Remembering that day makes me feel so protected. She was comforting me after I had fallen, landing hard, but unharmed from that big tree in the yard. There is no doubt that she loved and protected me. Something moved me to flip the photo over. There I read a brief note from my mother.

I will always love and protect the love of my life. My son Marlon Lakestone. Your mother.

Suddenly, like being struck by a bolt of lightning my body is tingling all over. Oh God! I feel total awareness that I suddenly know I'm listening to a guidance inside me like an alarm going off. Instinct has alerted me.

Is this what has been occurring in me these last few days? All those damn dreams. Times I've felt like my sanity was vulnerable. All I know, is that Ma is in some unknown danger. Ma and my wife are in danger. I must go find them. NOW!

I wished that I could be instantly walking into Fedco right now and not driving in this traffic. Calm down! Calm down! I can't be in a car accident. They have to be okay. Why didn't I tell Zena not to leave the house when I made that deal with her? I could have stopped it then. But I just didn't know then, or maybe I wasn't tuned in. I hadn't heeded the warning. It is loud and clear now like a silent alarm has sounded inside me. And here I am dealing with this traffic. SHIT! Calm down! Calm down! Changing lanes is not helping. I'm just about in the same spot regardless.

Just a few more blocks and I can connect with La Brea Ave which will be the fastest northbound street to get close to Fedco, before turning west to reach La Cienega Blvd. La Brea at this location is like driving through a canyon. On each side of the street is the high Baldwin Hills hamlet, with all the mansions looking down oblivious to the traffic. It looks like everybody is going the same way I'm going. But, when hasn't La Brea been congested and loaded with traffic.

Okay, okay! I'm on La Brea. It's 11:15 P.M. Please be all right. Just let me get there. I'm going to grab and hug them. Come on God. Help me. Please help me. Usually this part of La Brea goes pretty fast downhill from Stocker to Coliseum. Seems like it is about a mile down to Coliseum. But it is going unusually slow. Please don't let it be an accident. That would hold up everything. At this point, there isn't a way to turn off in this canyon of cars. We are all just creeping along. This would have to happen now. Come on. Just let me make it to Coliseum and I can turn off west. This must be it. Why is there water flowing down La Brea. I didn't hear any fire trucks. That's unusual. Traffic is slowed down on both sides. I can't see anything causing it. But it is enough to slow and back-up the flow of traffic.

Panic feels like it wants to take over. I must keep my focus. But it is difficult knowing. Knowing that… I can't do anything. I just need to get there. I can see the bottom of the hill and much, more water on the street. Does this have anything to do with the feeling of danger I'm sensing? It's certainly not helping me to reach them. This is all so overwhelming. I feel emotion welling up. No! I'm not panicking over this. Man up Marlon. You can do this. But God please help me.

I finally reach Coliseum, where the intersection is full of water that has flowed from somewhere. That panic is still there seeing that Coliseum and Rodeo Road are too congested to turn left to reach La Cienega and Fedco. Rodeo Road would take me right to the Fedco parking lot. Jefferson is my last option to head west. Traffic is heavy on every major artery today. What is it? If only I had a way to have a nexus with Ma and Zena. Even if I could, how would they react if I said you are in danger. How unusual and out of the ordinary that would be. But I want to be with them right now. That would be enough. The sensation is so powerful. I'm so close with just a few blocks to go, but so far still from reaching them. All right! All right I'm making progress.

Feeling accomplishment turning onto Jefferson only to find the same frustrating slow, moving traffic. Jefferson will take me just north of Fedco by a few blocks. If only this traffic would move. Nothing is going right. Stop! I'm tapping into fear and doubt, projecting apprehension rather than knowing my instincts guide me forward. I must trust, although these obstacles are so overwhelming at this point. I know I can do this. I can do this!

There are red flashing lights up ahead. No wonder traffic is slowed up. There is an accident a block or two ahead. That's it. What the hell? I'm parking right here in this No Parking Anytime Zone. That leaves me jogging the rest of the way on Jefferson. I'm out of shape so it's more walk, run. Walk run. I can smell that sweet aroma of candy being cooked at the famous See's Candy factor right up on La Cienega. Any other day I would rejoice taking in the sugary aroma, but right now I'm focused on getting to Ma and Zena.

The accident involving a delivery truck and two cars is right in the intersection of Jefferson and La Cienega. Traffic is at a stand-still going north and south. Man! I'm so glad I decided to abandon my car and run as much as I can tolerate. I bet Ma has a shopping cart brimming with Christmas gifts, household supplies, and lots of impulsive items to buy that she really doesn't need. She is enjoying it. So, what. Zena's has less in her cart, but there is lots of trim-the-tree items for the house. She never stops decorating. Just like Ma. They encourage each other. I love them so much. I need to feel them in my arms. I start running faster as I pass See's Candy. The Fedco sign is in view, stimulating me to use a burst of adrenaline to speed up.

Finally, stumbling into the store, while gasping for my breath, I seek to settle myself. My legs ache and tremble, my lungs are burning, and I'm wet with sweat. A security guard looks at me with suspicion and seems to be preparing for the worst, as if he needs to subdue me. Slowing my moves, standing up straight, and breathing much better, I calculate my next action. There is only one option. I must find Ma and my wife in this crazy store filled with frantic shoppers. The customer service station has a long line. I was hoping I could have them paged Zena. That won't work. Those people in line want their problems solved first. How about looking at the check-out lines. Maybe they are ready to get out of here. That would be perfect, but they are not in twenty extra long lines. What about running up and down the aisles and hollering their names? No way. That guard still has his eyes on me. I should seek his help and describe them. He may help.

"Hey man! Do you know how many people are in here right now? I'm not keeping track of nobody's family."

I'm feeling that fear inside again. There's nothing left but to run around searching for them. I'm bound to run into them. This is a huge store. But I am going to do this. Let me go to the...

"Mar?... You're here?!"

Oh my God! Zena found me. Not speaking, I just grab and hug her.

"What wrong Marlon? You look…" "Where is Ma? We have to go!"
"She was right behind me. Go? Go where? What's wrong Marlon? You look worried, or something." "Come on help me find Ma. We have to get out of here NOW!" "What? Marlon, I have all this stuff to pay for, and…"

"Zena, it is just stuff we can get it later. Please! I'm serious babe. We have to leave."

I understand how Zena must be feeling with me coming across this way, but I can't stop and comfort her. She is rushing behind me still pushing the cart with all her planned purchases. She is still rattling off questions and starting to alarm herself. Suddenly, as I turn the corner I bump into Ma. She looks just as surprised, but she doesn't say anything. Our eyes meet and communicate. I grab and embrace her close and strong. Her calm demur surprises me, but I shouldn't expect anything otherwise from her. It seems like a long moment that we hold each other. She snuggles her head next to mine and whispers in my ear.

"It's going to be all right Marlon. Whatever you are experiencing … I can feel your heart pounding against me baby. I can feel the energy racing through you. What is it you need me to do?"

I slowly push out of the embrace and look with intent purpose into her eyes again. I tell her that I'm feeling a strong instinctual message that they are in harm's way and that we must leave the store right now. She does not protest or question, still staring into my eyes. She turns and puts her arm around Zena's shoulders to calm the agitation and panic. Zena is tearing up, is very flush, and still clutches the cart with her stuff. She is caught between an overwhelming need to strongly protest and melting into a paralyzing bewildered ignorance of the present tense. She is internally questioning what to do with the heavy unfamiliarity of the situation enveloping her.

"Marlon let's go. Lead the way. Come on Zena. Hold my hand. Lord protect us all."

We manage our way through the crowded store and pass the same security guard that pondered about me when I entered. Now with eye brows raised and his mouth wide open, he watches us quickly exit to the parking lot. The parking lot is chaotic, swarming with cars and people coming and going. Horns blaring and a hum of inflated tires on busy La Cienega Blvd maintaining its usual urgency. The air is very still as if it is stifled and lacks the will to circulate. This is an ambivalent but somewhat typical Los Angeles winter day at slightly cool 68 degrees. The surprising clear sky offers a brilliant sun, searching for its zenith. But the sky is not typical. There is a low flying news coverage helicopter besides those of the LAPD surveying the area especially Baldwin Hills. In the distance numerous sirens become increasingly prominent. Suddenly, it is no longer a typical day.

I didn't need to ask Ma where to find her car. She always parks in about the same space near the very back of the lot. We all jolt into the roomy front seat, with Zena sitting in the middle. Ma never owned a small car, considering how small she is. She hands me the keys. I quickly bull doze my way into the westbound traffic of Rodeo Road. There is too much congestion to attempt the regular driving route to reach Ma's home in View Park. I won't feel we are protected until we reach her peaceful living room.

I can feel the tremble in Zena's body with her arm settles against me, as I drive faster than I should, weaving in and out of traffic. Without warning she pounds her hands on the padding above the dash board. She screams at the top of her lungs with shearing abandonment.

"Marlon! Stop the car right now! I mean it. Stop the damn car now! I can't take this. What the hell is going on? What is happening to us? Tell me! Tell me! Say something! This is crazy Ma. Why is he doing this to us? Why did we have to leave like that? Why are you driving so crazy Marlon? How can you not explain yourself, and not tell me what's going on? He said we had to leave now, didn't he Ma? I need to know. I need to know right NOW! I'm not crazy…this is crazy. CRAZY!"

The fear and panic are palpable in the car affecting each of us. It's all on me, but how do I explain the feelings and intuitions driving me as if I'm insane. I don't have the coinage to explain in the reality of Ma and my wife. I wish they could plug into my mind. I just can't stop driving and give a logical and believable explanation. For I have none. I don't know exactly what is about to happen. I just know we need to be away from here and secure in Ma's house. What if I said I think the world is coming to an end? Would that make her feel better? Hell no! But that's how it feels and what is forcing me into these bizarre actions and thoughts.

Ma puts her arms around Zena and pulls her close as she continues to cry softly. Ma talks calmly to her telling her that I wouldn't allow anything to happen to us. She says we must trust Marlon if he feels this strongly about this thing. This happening. This premonition he has.

"Baby I'm worried too. But I know my son wouldn't let anything so terrible happen to us. I trust him. and I know you do too honey. He must feel we are in some kind of danger. He loves you and wants to protect you. Be still and let the spirit of God wash over us, shield us."

I continue driving erratically as Ma hums softly and rocks Zena in her arms. After a tumultuous drive, we finally pull up in the driveway of Ma's home on Playa Vista Drive. They rush into the house. I stand at the entryway looking up and northward as I strain to hear sirens. I feel accomplished achieving the goal of our safety. I stand outside for a moment, but I'm far from feeling settled. There is still foreboding in the ethers.

I'm startled hearing Zena scream my name from inside the house. I turn to enter, and Ma meets me telling me to come quick to look at what is being broadcasted on the television. I sit down on the sofa next to Zena, while Ma settles next to me. The television volume is very loud for some reason. I guess Zena didn't want to risk missing anything being broadcasted by the KTLA special bulletin reporter. Zena slowly takes hold of my hand and holds it softly while rubbing it with her other hand. Ma scoots up next to me. We are all sitting on the edge of the sofa. Ma announces she is going to make a pot of tea. Zena ask if we might have something stronger. I focus on what the reporter is saying and the live shots of what is happening at the Baldwin Hills Reservoir. I have been stretched to my vulnerable limits over the last three days, and not a soul knew what I was going through. Some sense of peace is coming over me as I continue to look and listen.

The reporter indicates that a major catastrophic event was occurring at the Baldwin Hills reservoir. It started with a problem with the drainage system discovered by Los Angeles Department of Water and Power. It was the maintenance workers who heard water running. Just a trickle at first, the astonished reporter said. The maintenance workers described it as just a gurgling sound that turned into rumbling below the ground. That was sometime after 10:00 A.M. Nearing 12:00 noon things changed drastically. The department realized the wall holding back millions of gallons of water was in jeopardy and there was nothing they could do to avert a destructive disaster unseen in Los Angeles history. Their only hope was to release the water into the nearby Ballona Creek to avoid loss of lives and homes. The police and fire department began an urgent effort to evacuate the homes below the reservoir including the large community known as Village Green, and Fedco, the large shopping center filled with Christmas shoppers. They ran from house to house knocking on doors, while LAPD helicopters sounded warnings from above.

"Oh my God… Look at that… JESUS!"

Ma reacted to the helicopter shot on the television of the reservoir water breaching the wall and rushing down the northern side of Baldwin Hills. It was a huge flow of water, mud and debris rumbling with such force, taking the path of Cloverdale Avenue, overtaking Village Green and major streets including La Brea, Coliseum, Rodeo Road, Jefferson, and La Cienega. Most of the homes on Cloverdale were destroyed, eroded off their foundations. The Village Green area is overwhelmed with fast rushing water, filled with mud, trees, and cars. The pathway of obliteration is cruel and final.

"Oh no… Look Mar. That's Fedco where you found me and Zena… My goodness! Look at all that water. That could have been us trying to escape. Those poor people."

The Fedco parking lot was inundated with flood water. As the helicopter flew over the lot, frantic shoppers appear terrified, confused, and uncertain about their situations as they try to navigate in the waist deep water. The reporter noted that the interior of Fedco was being flooded while shoppers and store staff are still inside. Across from Fedco people were rushing out of the Rodeo Bowl, a bowling alley which was also being flooded.

The KTLA TV helicopter helped police and fire department workers locate citizens trapped in trees, on roof tops of homes, apartments, and businesses, trapped in floating cars, all along the swath of liquefied destruction. The reporter expresses pronounced emotion, describing the camera focusing in on a car that was swallowed into a caved in chasm eight feet deep in the street. A woman struggles in the car as it fills with the muddy debris loaded water.

"Oh wow! Look at that Zena. Poor lady. That looks so nightmarish, but it is real." "Mar. I'm so sorry about the way I acted… That was terrible when I exploded on you. I'm sorry." "It's all right babe. You had no way of knowing. I didn't know really myself exactly what the danger was. I just knew that my love for you and Ma was the greatest driving force that kept telling me what I had to do. To tell the truth over the last two days I've been overwhelmed with thoughts, scary dreams, and premonitions… And you know what Ma? Pops has been with me throughout this. You know how he was. How wise he was, and especially how connected he was with his spirit." "Yes baby. You are blessed." "I regret I let my fear overtake me. I wished that I would have just been still and listened. I guess I looked like I was crazy. I felt like I was losing my mind. But I'm here and so are you two. I regret that I couldn't prevent the whole thing."

"Wait a minute now Marlon. How many times have you heard me say everything happens for a reason? And there are no mistakes between interactions of souls, because your soul knows what it knows because it is supposed to. It is just supposed to, and you are to believe it fully. I have heard both of you say I had a gut reaction, or what does your gut say. We have forgotten what we know. We talked about this Marlon. And stop using those disparaging words to describe yourself. Your reality is what you speak. What would have happened if you had told Zena she couldn't go to Fedco because it was going to be flooded by the reservoir? She would have given you that look and probably said, quite talking crazy. She may have even asked what reservoir! If you would have called 911 would they have gone to Fedco or to your house to question you? If you told the security guard on duty to evacuate the store immediately because a flood was coming would he have called 911, or called for back-up because he had an irrational customer in the store? The important thing is that you eventually knew what to do and you did your very best to accomplish protecting your family.... It was all about love Marlon."

"Yeah Ma. I love you two and wouldn't let a thing harm you or Zena. Thanks for planting your wisdom on it to help me better comprehend what I have been going through. We can see that people are suffering as we talk right now. Many won't have a place to sleep tonight."

"Mar. I just have to say I'm sorry again. I'm grateful to be here next to you in this house. And thank you too Ma." "But why are you crying Zena?" "It is all so sad to see… All this nice, sweet talk is okay, but I haven't had time to collect myself yet. This whole thing did something to me. I felt so vulnerable, and helpless. I didn't have time to understand. You know? Nothing was real for me and it got worse the more you couldn't make clear to me what was happening. You just said come on, come on we must go NOW! And Ma nothing bothers you. I mean not a thing. How did you stay so calm? That made me feel like something was wrong with me. You didn't have not one question. Not a single why. There was no pausing for you… How?… Okay… I'm so glad to have both of you to love and be loved by, but my spirituality and faith is nothing like what y'all have. I felt so alone through what was happening. Even sitting right next to you. I had no control over myself and"

"Aw baby. Don't cry. Come here and let me hug you Zena. Love is the only answer I have for today, and to explain how we are sitting here together right now. I saw the worse that could have happened. Know I would never let anything hurt you. You are too valuable to me. Go ahead and cry and feel better. I'm right her babe."

"Zena. You know you are my girl. My baby girl. I love you as my natural daughter. There is nothing I wouldn't do for you. I hope you know that sweetie." "I know Ma. Thank you."

"There is just one last thing for me to know. And let's all laugh together about it... We all rode home in Ma's car, right? But, where is my car?"

Conclusion

A few days later Marlon Lakestone sits across from his boss Mr. Jackson's as he sorts through papers on his desk. Mr. Jackson is the Biltmore Hotel manager.   He looks up and smiles at Marlon and speaks about how pleased he was with the way Marlon handle the crisis during the large conference that took place a few days ago. He complements Marlon by saying he likes the way he handles people and situations in a compassionately calm but firm manner. He explains that the upcoming convention starting Thursday and lasting through the weekend will be just as challenging for the hotel. He tells Marlon that he expects the same professionalism from Marlon as in the previous week. The discussion ends with Marlon's assurance and Mr. Jackson's statement that they need to discuss Marlon's future with the Biltmore Hotel. Standing and smiling he extends his hand to shake Marlon's.

Marlon arrives in the hotel lounge to take his lunch and catches the KTLA news summary of the recent Baldwin Hills Reservoir disaster.

There were approximately 2000 victims, with 5 deaths occurring in the Village Green community immediately below the reservoir. Nearly 8000 people were unable to live in their homes. Damages and losses totaled well over ten million dollars. Surprisingly, the catastrophic event lasted less than six hours from the first signs of trouble until the destructive flash flooding turned into waves of water on the streets near the popular Fedco shopping center.

The reservoir was not as well known in Los Angeles as would be expected for its size and importance. The Los Angeles Department of Water and Power started constructed of the dam in 1947. The construction concluded in 1951.

Marlon's mother had shared information about the reservoir with him approximately a year prior. A community meeting was held at her church during which time an environmental group shared concerns about the effects of the Inglewood Oil Fields on La Cienega and the reservoir since both were located on the Newport-Inglewood Fault. The question was raised about the impact of a major earthquake occurring on the fault running directly in the areas of concern.

Civil engineers, and geologist were not 100% satisfied with studies and felt that the soil was unstable for a reservoir to have been built at the top of Baldwin Hills. During this time, the need for progressive technologies took precedence over geological studies. The need for an additional supply of water for Los Angeles spurred on the construction of the reservoir and lessened the geological considerations.

Epilogue

Marlon is living a very comfortable life as what he calls his true self. He is pleased and involved with his family, and profession. It has been fifteen years since he had so much difficulty with emotional episodes and lack of direction and stability in his career choices. He still talks about the flood at the Fedco shopping center, that dreadful day in December. He speaks freely about rescuing his mother and wife, after nightmares drove him into an astonishing knowingness.

He and his wife are the proud parents of a baby boy named Adam Lakestone II. They experienced a very painful period during which Zena had multiple miscarriages attempting to give birth to a baby. For her own health both physically and mentally her doctor recommended that they put off trying to get pregnant for a while. During this time, their marriage suffered as they went into a period of finger pointing and blaming.

The marriage began to crumble after Marlon decided to stop working a regular job and enrolled in college to pursue a degree in music composition and education. They became estranged and lived separately. Surprisingly, Zena moved in with Marlon's mother while he

165

maintained on his own. Ma in her infinite wisdom and spiritually astute ways, was very patient and encouraging with both of them.

Periodically, they would spend time together and appeared as if they were still the same loving couple. Other times they couldn't be in the same room together as they argued and acted like they despised each other. However, during one of their conjugal visits, Marlon rolled over beside Zena after intercourse becoming suddenly silent. Zena repeatedly attempted to get him to talk and explain what was going on. Slowly, he sat up and turned to look directly at Zena.

"Babe, I know right this moment, that you are going to be a mother. We are going to have our baby."

After much back and forth discussion about his profound statement, Marlon wanted Zena's belief.

"Trust me Zena. I know because I know. I wouldn't be foolish about something so serious considering what we have been through. And I love you babe as I always have."

True enough, a few weeks later, Zena's doctor confirmed that she was indeed pregnant. The doctor strongly urged her to reduce all activity as much as possible and confine herself to bed. Ma became her nurse and overseer of the doctor's orders. Marlon waited on her unceasingly, even cooking her meals and feeding her in bed.

The baby was born without complications and declared healthy and strong. Marlon and Zena were so happy and grateful for their baby boy. Ma prayed over all of them, thanking God for her grandson. Marlon was inseparable from his son, especially following the first birthday and baby Adam became more active.

"This little Adam is my only begotten son."

Zena was so proud and happy to finally give birth to a baby. She was also very proud of her husband who eventually, became a professor at the University of Southern California, where he taught Music History. His favorite subjects he enjoyed teaching were Composition, and Jazz Improvisations. Zena, Ma, and baby Adam were at every home football game to watch Marlon proudly conduct the USC Trojan Marching Band.

Marlon organized a jazz quartet in which of course, he plays the piano. The group performed at the very famous Dunbar Hotel on Central Avenue is South Los Angeles. The Dunbar was the epicenter for jazz and home for many well know black entertainment royalty during the jazz renaissance in Los Angeles. Some of the most famous to stay at the

Dunbar includes Duke Ellington, Lena Horne, Fats Waller, Billie Holiday, and Ella Fitzgerald.

The black entertainers were banned from staying in the white owned hotels where they performed nightly in Hollywood and other parts of Los Angeles. The Dunbar served as their homes while in Los Angeles. It was their station of solidarity and loyalty to each other, and the African American community.

Marlon became the President of the Central Avenue Hotel Dunbar Jazz Association, where he spearheaded efforts to reopen the Dunbar and bring jazz back to Central Avenue. Marlon also planned a trip to New Orleans for the Jazz association to attend a music symposium and Jazz Festival. Several of the members took their families with them on the trip as a vacation as did Marlon.

It was so exciting for Marlon to have Zena and Ma along with him, but especially his son Adam. The excitement was the result of his plan to take them all back to visit Holmes Mississippi. To visit Pops' land that he talked so much about with Zena. He wanted his baby boy to walk barefoot on the same dirt where he cavorted and toiled as a boy.

Marlon and Ma had ambivalent reactions during the Holmes sojourn. They stood silent in front of the big family house with the wrap around porch where they spend summer nights listening to Pops speak his wisdom and guidance. It was bitter sweet thinking about Stone playing the piano on hot summer nights. Weeds and over-grown vines surrounded the house. The house was leaning, ready to collapse on its side. The steps to the porch had collapsed and had rotted to thick splinters. It was difficult to distinguish the original color since the paint had chipped entirely, giving the appearance of fish scales on the ashen surface.

Everyone walked away from the house lead by Marlon carrying his son. They walked on without speaking. Only little Adam's constant talking, and curious questions could be heard. Pointed at everything and expected the usual responses from his father. Soon, they arrived at the hill where the huge majestic tree stood, that Pops planted. The tree's massive branches were cover with the colorful foliage that Marlon remembered from his boyhood days.

Marlon and Ma stop as they walked to Pops' grave marker underneath the tree. They paused contemplating their own private thoughts about the moment. The silence was broken when baby Adam pointed and said tree. Ma responded by telling Adam that yes, that's your tree baby.

Marlon out stretched his arms to embrace his family and said it is time.

"Time for us to go home."